THE BOOK OF SPLENDOURS

THE
BOOK
OF
SPLENDOURS

The Inner Mysteries of Qabalism

Its relationship to Freemasonry, Numerology & Tarot

Eliphas Levi

Appendix by Papus

Foreword by R.A. Gilbert

SAMUEL WEISER, INC.

York Beach, Maine

This edition published in 1984 by
Samuel Weiser, Inc.
Box 612
York Beach, Maine 03910-0612

99 98 97
11 10 9 8 7 6 5

First published in English in 1973
First paperback edition, 1981

Library of Congress Catalog Card Number: 84-214089

ISBN 0-87728-614-0
BJ

Printed in the United States of America

The paper used in this publication meets the minimum require-
ments of the American National Standard for Permanence of
Paper for Printed Library Materials Z39.48-1984.

CONTENTS

FOREWORD

I n his Introduction to the English translation, Dr Abelson describes the *Zohar* as 'the fundamental book of Jewish Cabbalism' and as 'the premier textbook of medieval Jewish mysticism'.[1] More than this, the *Zohar* is also, in the words of Denis Saurat, 'a strange mixture of the wildest tales obviously of folklore origin, at times without any philosophical meaning whatever, of the most extraordinary superstitions, of the most imaginative myths, and at times of the profoundest metaphysical conceptions'.[2]

Such a description could apply equally to the magical works of Eliphas Lévi, and it seems almost inevitable that the *Zohar* should have fascinated the enigmatic mind of Lévi, who saw in it a hidden wisdom unique to his vision, which he drew out and expounded at length—to the fury of scholars who, lacking his inner sight, saw it in a very different light. So, is there truly a hidden wisdom in the *Zohar,* and is it of such a pattern as Eliphas Lévi presents in his *Book of Splendours?*

The occultist will answer Yes, for with Lévi he will see the *Zohar* as a 'Masterpiece of the Occult Sciences', containing the lost knowledge of the ancient world. The scholar, however, lives in the real world and must judge the book by the more prosaic standards of the historian and literary critic.

Viewed objectively, the *Zohar* is a series of mystical commentaries on the Pentateuch, set in the form of discourses between Simeon ben Jochai, the Second Century Qabalistic Rabbi, and his disciples. It first appeared in written form in the late thirteenth century when it was transcribed by the Spanish Qabalist, Moses de Leon, who claimed that he had copied it from earlier manuscripts and that it was indeed the work of Simeon ben Jochai. The manuscript versions were followed by printed editions in Hebrew, first published at Mantua in Italy in 1558 and later throughout Europe, while translations have appeared in Latin, German, French and English. Until recent years it was considered that Moses de Leon had collected earlier material, both Jewish and non-Jewish, from oral sources and acted only as editor, but in his book *Major trends in Jewish Mysticism* (1941), Gershom Scholem showed convincingly and conclusively that Moses de Leon was the true author — and the sole author — of the *Zohar*. Simeon ben Jochai and high antiquity are alike displaced, which is, of course, anathema to the occultist.

But a false ascription of authorship need not condemn the content of a book: the *Zohar* is unquestionably among the greatest mystical works of all time, and has exercised a powerful influence on later mystics, both Jewish and Christian. It stresses above all the spirituality of man, the importance of the human soul and—the distinctive contribution of Qabalism to mystical thought—the manner in which the transcendent God becomes immanent through the emanation of the ten Sephiroth. It is this doctrine of the Sephiroth, with all its strange ramifications, that has appealed most to the occultist— and not least to Eliphas Lévi, who absorbed it in his soul and used it to work a strange transmutation on his own writings that has given them a lasting fascination.

And what of Eliphas Lévi — that 'Incarnated Paradox' as Madame Blavatsky called him?[3] What sort of man was it who could exert such an enormous influence not only in France but also upon all the major figures of the 'Occult Revival': on H.P. Blavatsky as well as on Anna Kingsford, on both Aleister Crowley and A. E. Waite?

Alphonse Louis Constant, to give him his real name, was

born in Paris in 1810, the son of a poor shoemaker. As a boy both his aptitude for learning and his religious fervour were apparent, so that he was considered an ideal candidate for the priesthood and at the age of fifteen commenced a ten-year seminary education during which he first began to develop his unorthodox ideas. In 1835 he was ordained Deacon, but he had realized that he could not accept the condition of celibacy and abandoned his calling before he was made a priest. Even so, the priesthood retained its hold upon him, and his ambivalent attitude to the Catholic Church seems to indicate a yearning for his lost vocation.

For some time after leaving the seminary Constant made a living by teaching and writing, but both occupations brought their problems: his teaching led him into a series of doubtful liaisons with female pupils, culminating in 1846 with his disastrous marriage to Noémi Cadiot (who left him seven years later), while his writing earned for him eight months in prison for his extreme brand of Christian Socialism as expressed in *La Bible de la Liberté* (1841). After that episode his writing was interrupted by a brief but vain attempt to return to his work in the Church, and resumed in even more inflammatory style until the Revolution in 1848 burned out his radical zeal and gave birth to the Magician.

Shortly after his seminary days, Constant's occult leanings had been awakened by his involvement with the self-styled prophet and pseudo-Messiah, Ganneau, and in 1852 he met an even more remarkable prophet, the *émigré* and Polish mystic, Hoene Wronski (1778-1853). Under Wronski's influence Constant began his first major work, *Dogme et Rituel de la Haute Magie,* which was published in 1856 under the pseudonym he was to use for the rest of his life: Eliphas Lévi.[4] This amazing book was followed by the equally remarkable *Histoire de la Magie* (1861)[5] and by a dozen others, most of which were not published until after Lévi's death in 1875.

During the twenty years of his occult career Lévi's fame spread and his disciples multiplied, attracted both by the man and by his teachings, which were at once profound, original

and infuriating, for assuredly Magic had never been so
overwhelmed by its own glamour as in its history and doctrines
according to Eliphas Lévi. And yet, despite their eccentricities
and distortions, his works survive and still fascinate. Why?

Here we come to the heart of the problem and the heart of
the man. Lévi was no armchair occultist, but a living Magus
who believed in his work and in himself; and the centre of his
work was the Qabalah—altered, to be sure, and moulded into a
quasi-Christian framework, but still the Qabalah. So Lévi
produced his *Livre des Splendeurs*, for what is at the heart of
the Qabalah save the *Zohar*? Admittedly, the text is mis-
labelled (for he was translating the *Idra Rabba*, not the *Idra
Zuta* as he claimed), arbitrarily abridged and outrageously
explained; but it remains a delight, for he crystallized in it not
the true meaning of the Qabalah but the essence of the
occultist's *interpretation* of it.

When it was finally published, in 1894, the *Livre des
Splendeurs* had become more of an anthology of Lévi's work,
for it contains, in addition to the Zoharic extract, the essence
of his Qabalistic ideas (in the *Qabalistic Lessons*), his self-
revealing *Profession of Faith* and the careful analysis of his
doctrines by his disciple and spiritual heir, Papus (Gérard
Encausse, 1865-1916). This analysis is especially important as
it comprises the only reasoned, contemporary opinion of Lévi's
work that is readily accessible, for Waite's critical introduction
to *The Mysteries of Magic* has long been virtually
unobtainable.[6]

Recent opinions of Eliphas Lévi have been as ambivalent as
were those of his own day and reflect the perplexing nature of
this enigmatic man. Even Waite, who studied him more
closely than did any self-styled occultist before or since, was
baffled by Lévi but gave him a fitting epitaph: 'He is the most
brilliant, the most original, the most fascinating interpreter of
occult philosophy in the West.[7] And so he remains, for in the
century since his death no-one has emerged to claim his
mantle.

R. A. Gilbert
Bristol, June 1981

NOTES

1. *The Zohar,* translated by Harry Sperling and Maurice Simon (Soncino Press, 1931-1934), Vol. 1, p.ix.
2. Denis Saurat, *Blake and Modern Thought* (Constable, 1929), p.99.
3. H. P. Blavatsky, *The Secret Doctrine* (T.P.H., 1893), Vol. 2, p.617.
4. Eliphas Lévi Zahed is the supposed Hebraic form of Alphonse Louis Constant.
5. Translated as *The History of Magic* (Rider, 1913) by A. E. Waite, who also translated the *Dogme et Rituel,* as *Transcendental Magic* (Rider, 1923).
6. The best modern study of Lévi's life and work is Christopher McIntosh's *Eliphas Lévi and the French Occult Revival* (Rider, 1972).
7. *The Mysteries of Magic. A Digest of the writings of Eliphas Lévi.* With a biographical and critical Essay by Arthur Edward Waite (Kegan Paul, 1897), p.xiii.

PREFACE

Judaism is the oldest, the most rational and the truest of religions.

Jesus, who set himself the task of reforming Judaism, never advised his disciples to abandon it. The reform of Jesus, unacceptable to the heads of the synagogue whose legitimate authority was never contested by the Christian master, has become a heresy which has invaded the entire world.

At first mistreated by the Jews, the Christians, once the power was theirs, outlawed and persecuted the Jews with the most shameful and cowardly assiduity. Their books were burned instead of being studied, and the precious philosophy of the Hebrews was lost to the Christian world.

The apostles, however, were correct in their feeling that the Gentile ministry would last only so long and that the new faith would one day weaken. Then, they said, salvation will come again to us from Israel, and the great religious revolution that will reunite us with our fathers will be as a passage from death to life.

The Hebrews are in possession of a science whose existence St Paul suspected and which St John, initiated by Jesus, both hid and revealed within the immense hieroglyphs of the Apocalypse, borrowing for the most part from the prophecy of Ezekiel. There exists a shadowy and wonderous book entitled the Sohar or Splendour. This huge book, larger than the Talmud, is however nothing more than the development of a theogony in several pages, called the *Siphra Dzeniûta.*

On this book, brought back to us from the Orient by Guillaume Postel, we give the magnificent Commentary of Rabbi Simeon Ben-Jochai, to which we will also add the principal legends of Masonic tradition, borrowed in their entirety from the Qabalah of the Hebrews.

Solomon's temple was, to be sure, a wholly symbolical edifice. Its plan, its construction, its ornaments, its vessels, all represented a synthesis of all sciences. It was the universe, it was philosophy, it was the heavens. Solomon laid down the plans. Hiram executed them with perfect understanding, the directors of work were well-versed in the science of detail, the workers followed closely the plans of the masters. This hierarchy, so rational and just, is taken in Freemasonry to represent the model of a perfect society. Freemasonry is eclectic, independent Judaism. The Freemasons wish to rebuild the temple, in other words, to re-establish a primitive society based on this meaningful hierarchy and on progressive initiation, without the obstacles of priests and kings; it is for this reason they call themselves Freemasons, free builders.

The publication of this work will make known the implacable hate borne by priests of Catholicism towards Freemasonry, which is Judaism reformed according to the thought of Jesus and his beloved apostle, John, whose Qabalistic revelation has always been the gospel of occult Christianity and the schools of unprofaned Gnosticism. Associated with these schools are the Johannites, the non-idolatrous Templars and the advanced initiates of occult Masonry. It is there that the keys of the future are to be found, for there are preserved the secrets of the single, universal revelation whose doctrines Judaism, first and perhaps singly among religions, has preached to the world.

One God, one people, one science, one law, one faith,

one king. This is the view of Judaism which still awaits its temple and its Messiah.

'When will the Messiah come?' asked Rabbi Simeon of the prophet Elijah who often came down from heaven to speak with the master of the Sohar. 'This very day,' answered the prophet. 'Go to the gate of Rome and you will see.' Rabbi Simeon went to the gate of Rome, remained there all day, then came away, having seen nothing more than a number of beggars covered with sores and a stranger, poor in appearance, who consoled them and ministered to their wounds. Once home, he found Elijah there and said: 'Master, why have you mocked your servant?' 'But I have not deceived you,' said the prophet. 'Did you not see a man performing works of charity? Well, I say to you that the reign of charity is the Messiah's reign, and if you wish for the coming of the Messiah every day, then perform charity every day.'

Charity, according to the apostle St John, is the substance and the final goal of Christianity.

Charity, according to St Paul, is all that cannot fail to outlast unfulfilled prophecies and outmoded knowledge.

Charity, in the words of this same apostle, is greater than hope and faith.

Christians who curse the Jews by calling them murderers of God, and Jews who scorn Christians by calling them idolaters, disobey in like manner the tenets of their religion, which preaches charity.

Charity is the deep and active awareness of the human community.

Judaism should lend Freemasonry a brotherly hand, for the profession of faith of all non-atheistic Masons is the symbol of Maimonides; Christians must recognize in the performance of the advanced rites all the allegorical revelation of Jesus Christ.

In Freemasonry the wedding, the fusion of Qabalistic Judaism and the neo-Platonic Christianity of St John is an accomplished fact. Already there exists in the world a universal Israelite alliance which welcomes the adhesion of upright men from all religions and whose president is, at the time of writing, the Hon. Monsieur Crémieux. The great rabbi Isidor is a partisan of progress, of reform and of free thought. Enlightened Jews render homage to the morality of the Gospels, as enlightened Christians recognize the wisdom and profundity of the Talmud's teachings; science and free thought bring together those that heretofore fanaticism divided. Study of the Qabalah will unite as a single people both Israelites and Christians.

It is in vain that ignorance and fanaticism would perpetuate war; peace is already outlined in the name of philosophy, and soon it will be established by religion, liberated at last from the domination of human passions.

It is in preparation for this great event that we must make known to knowledgeable men the hidden magnificence of Judaic wisdom. For this reason we publish the translation and explication of the theogony of the Sohar contained in the *Siphra Dzeniûta*. It will be seen what masters they were, these rabbis of the great Qabalistic school. There is nothing stranger or more beautiful than the great synod whose deliberations are set down in the book of the *Idra Suta*.

There is nothing occult which should not be made manifest, Jesus said, and that which was only whispered from ear to ear should be shouted from the rooftops.

For, as he adds elsewhere, light was not made to be hid under a bushel; but on the contrary, it must shine from a candlestick, lighting the way for all who are in the house.

The house of humanity is the world; the candlestick is science; and the light is reason, enlivened and immortalized by faith.

Part One

The Idra Suta
or The Great Synod

Commentary on the Siphra Dzeniúta
by Simeon Ben-Jochai

I

Jerusalem had just been destroyed by the Romans. It was forbidden to the Jews, on pain of death, to return to mourn the ruins of their homeland. The entire nation had been dispersed, the holy traditions lost. The true Qabalah had given way to puerile and superstitious subtleties. Those who claimed to preserve the heritage of hidden doctrine were nothing more than sorcerers and fortune-tellers, justly proscribed by the laws of nations. It was then that a venerable rabbi named Simeon Ben-Jochai gathered round him the last initiates of primitive science, having resolved to explain to them the book of high theogony called the Book of Mystery. Each of them knew the text by heart, but only the rabbi Simeon was acquainted with the profound meaning of this book which had, up to this time, been transmitted from mouth to mouth, from memory to memory, without explication or even benefit of the written word.

In order to assemble them round him, here are the words he sent them:

'Why, in these days of great torment, should we remain as a house supported by a single column, or as a man who stands on only one foot? It is time to take action for the Lord, for men have lost the true sense of the law.

'Our days grow short, the master calls; the harvest has

been abandoned, the reapers have strayed far from the ripened vine.

'Come together in this same countryside where so much has so lately gone undone. Come, as if for combat, armed with wisdom, counsel, intelligence, knowledge and attention; let your feet be as unencumbered as your hands.

'Acknowledge as your only master he who holds sway over life and death, and together we shall utter the words of truth which heaven's saints are wont to hear, and they will come down among us to hear us.'

On the appointed day, the rabbis assembled in the fields, in a circular space enclosed by a high wall.

They arrived in silence. Rabbi Simeon sat down in the midst of them, and seeing them all together, he wept.

'I am lost,' he cried, 'if I reveal the great mysteries! I am lost if I leave them unexplained!'

The rabbis remained silent.

At last one of them, named Rabbi Abba, spoke, saying:

'With the master's permission. Is it not written: "The secrets of the Lord belong to those who fear him"? And all we who are here, do we not fear the Lord, and are we not already privy to the secrets of the Temple?'

Now here are the names of those who were present: Rabbi Eleazar, son of Rabbi Simeon, Rabbi Abba, Rabbi Jehuda, Rabbi José, son of Jacob, Rabbi Isaac, Rabbi Thiskia, son of Raf, Rabbi José and Rabbi Jesa.

All, binding themselves to secrecy, put their hand in that of Rabbi Simeon and with him pointed towards heaven. Then they took their seats in the circumscribed area, where they were well hidden by large trees.

Rabbi Simeon stood and prayed; then he sat down again and said to them: 'Come, all of you, and place your right hand on my breast.'

They did so; and he, taking all these hands in his own, said solemnly: 'Cursed be he who makes for himself an idol and hides it! Woe unto him who covers falsehood with the veils of mystery!'

The eight rabbis answered: 'Amen.'

Rabbi Simeon went on: 'There is only one true God, before whom no other gods exist, and there is only one true people, the body of those who worship the one true God.'

Then he called his son Eleazar and had him seat himself before him. Near him, he placed Rabbi Abba and said: 'We now form a triangle, the primordial figure of all that exists; we represent the door of the temple and its two columns.'

Rabbi Simeon then refrained from speaking, and his disciples likewise. An obscure murmur made itself heard, like that of a large gathering. It was the spirits of heaven who had come down to listen.

The disciples trembled, but Rabbi Simeon said to them: 'Fear nothing and rejoice. For it is written: "Lord, I have heard the sound of your presence and I trembled."'

'Formerly God ruled over man through fear, but now his reign is that of love. Has it not been said: "You shall love your God"? And did he not himself say: "I have loved you"?'

Then he added: 'The secret doctrine is for reflective souls; the troubled and restless soul cannot understand it. Can one have confidence in a nail fixed to a moving wall, ready as it is to crumble at the slightest shock?

'The whole world is founded on mystery, and if discretion is necessary in worldly affairs, how much greater should be our reserve when dealing with the mysterious dogmas which God does not even reveal to the highest of his angels?

'Heaven bends down to listen to us, but my words must remain veiled. The earth moves in order to hear, but what I say will be in symbols.

'We are, at this very moment, the gate and the columns of the universe.'

At last Rabbi Simeon spoke, and tradition preserved in the mystery of mysteries assures us that when he opened his mouth, the earth trembled beneath his feet and that his disciples felt its trembling.

II

He spoke first of the kings who ruled over Edom before the coming of the king Israel, symbols of the unbalanced powers which manifested themselves at the beginning of the universe, before the triumph of harmony.

'God,' said he, 'when he wished to create, threw over his radiance a veil and in its folds, he cast his shadow. From this shadow there arose giants who said: "We are kings": but they were nothing more than phantoms. They appeared because God had hidden himself by creating night within chaos; they disappeared when there was brought forth in the east that luminous head, that glowing head that humanity gives itself by proclaiming the existence of God, the sun, governor of our aspirations and our thoughts.

'The gods are mirages made of shadow, and God is the synthesis of splendours. Usurpers fall away when the king mounts his throne, and when God appears, the gods are banished.'

III

'Thus, when God had permitted the night to exist, in order that the stars might appear, he turned towards the shadow he had made and considered it, to give it a face.

'He formed an image on the veil with which he had covered his glory, and this image smiled at him, and he regarded this image as his own, so that he might create man in accordance with it.

'In a manner of speaking, he tried out this prison reserved for created spirits. He looked at this face that was to become one day the face of man, and his heart was moved, for already he seemed to hear the lamentations of his creations.

'You who wish to subject me to the law, it seemed to say, give me proof that this law is just, by subjecting yourself to it as well.

'And so God became man in order that he might be loved and understood by men.

'Now, of him we know only this image, formed on the veil which hides his splendour. This image is our own, and he wishes that we recognize it to be also his.

'Thus we know him without knowing him; he shows us a form and possesses none. We have given him the image of an old man, he who has no age.

'He is seated on a throne from which escape eternally sparks of light by the millions, and he commands them to become worlds. His hair radiates and stirs the stars. Universes revolve around his head, and suns bathe themselves in his light.'

IV

'The divine image is a double one. There are the heads of light and of shadow, the white ideal and the black ideal, the upper head and the lower. One is the dream of the Man-God, the other is the invention of the God-Man. One represents the God of the wise, and the other, the idol of the lowly.

'All light, in truth, implies shadow and possesses its brilliance only in opposition to that shadow.

'The luminous head pours out upon the dark one a constant dew of splendour. "Let me in, my beloved," says God to intelligence, "for my head is filled with dew, and among the curls of my hair wander the tears of night."

'This dew is the manna by which the souls of the just are nourished. The elect are hungry for it and gather it abundantly in the fields of heaven.

'These drops are round pearls, brilliant as diamonds and clear as crystal. They are white and glow with all colours, for there is one simple truth alone: the splendour of all things.'

V

'The divine image has thirteen rays: four on each side of the triangle in which we enclose it and one at its uppermost point.

'Draw it in the sky with your thought, trace its lines from star to star, it will contain three hundred and sixty multitudes of worlds.

'For the high old one called the Macroprosopopeia or the great creative hypothesis is also called Arich-Anphin, the immense countenance. The other, the human god, the face of shadow, the Microprosopopeia, the limiting hypothesis, is called Seir-Anphin or the contracted countenance.

'When this countenance beholds the face of light, it grows and becomes harmonious. Order is thus restored; but this cannot last, for the thoughts of man are as changeable as man himself.

'But there is always a luminous thread which attaches shadow to light. This thread runs through the innumerable conceptions of human thought, linking them all to divine splendour.

'The head of light sends out its whiteness to all thinking heads or entities, when they follow the path of law and reason.'

VI

'The head of the supreme old one is a closed receptacle, where infinite wisdom lies at rest like a fine wine whose lees cannot be disturbed.

'This wisdom is impenetrable, possessor of itself in

silence within eternity, inaccessible to the vicissitudes of time.

'It is the light, but it is the dark head which is the lamp. The oil of intelligence is meted out, and its brilliance, by thirty-two ways, is made manifest.

'God revealed is God hidden. This human shadow of God is like the mysterious Eden from which there issued a spring that divided itself into four rivers.

'Nothing pours forth from God himself. His substance is without issue. Nothing departs from him and nothing enters in, for he is impenetrable and immutable. All that begins, all that appears, all that is divided, all that flows and passes, begins, appears, is divided, flows and passes in his shadow. He is, unto himself, immovable in his light, and he remains thus, like an old wine laid to rest.'

VII

'Do not seek to penetrate the thoughts of the mysterious head. Its intimate thoughts are hidden, but its exterior, creative thoughts shine forth like a head of hair. White hair without shadow and whose strands are never tangled.

'Each strand is a thread of light attached to millions of worlds. The hairs are divided at the forehead and descend on either side; but each side is the right side. For in the divine image which constitutes this head of light, the left side has no place.

'The left side of the head of light is the dark head, for in traditional symbolism, the lower reaches are the equivalent of the left.

'Now, between the heights and the depths of the image of God there must be no more antagonism than between the left hand and right hand of man, since harmony results from the analogy of opposites.

'Israel in the desert grew discouraged and asked: "Is God with us or against us?"'

'Thus they spoke of him whom one knows and of him who is not known.

'Thus they separated the white head from the dark head.

'The god of shadow became, then, an exterminating phantom.

'They were punished because they had doubted through lack of confidence and love.

'One does not understand God, but one loves him; and it is love that produces faith.

'God hides from the mind of man, but reveals himself to the heart.

'When man says: "I do not believe in God," it is as if he were to say: "I do not love."

'And the voice of shadow answers: "You will die because your heart renounces life."

'The Microprosopopeia is the great night of faith, and it is in faith that the just live and breathe. They stretch forth their hands and take hold of the hair of the father, and from these splendid strands fall drops of light which come to illuminate their night.

'Between the two sides of these divided strands is the pathway of initiation, the middle path, the path of opposites in harmony.

'There, all is reconciled and understood. There, only good triumphs and evil is no longer.

'This pathway is that of supreme balance and is called the last judgment of God.

'The hairs of the white head spread out in perfect order on all sides, but do not cover the ears.

'For the ears of the Lord are always open to prayer. And nothing can prevent them from hearing the orphan's cry or the wail of the oppressed.'

THE COLLOQUY

I

On the forehead of the supreme head resides the majesty of majesties, the goodness of all goodnesses united, the true pleasure of all true pleasures.

'This is love, whose power is created and shared by all those who love.

'Humanity's will, symbolized by the forehead of the Microprosopopeia, must correspond to this love.

'The forehead of collective man is called Reason. It is often veiled in shadow, but when it shows itself, God gives ear to the prayers of Israel. When, then, does it show itself?'

Rabbi Simeon paused a moment, then reiterated his question: 'Yes, when?'

And turning toward Rabbi Eleazar, his son, he repeated: 'When does it show itself?'

'At the time of common prayer on the day of the Lord,' answered Rabbi Eleazar.

'How?' asked the master.

'Men, when they pray, prostrate themselves before God whom they imagine as angry; the forehead of the head of shadow is then covered with clouds and it seems that thunder and lightning must issue from them.

'But the shadows part, struck by a ray from the supreme face: eternal serenity imprints its image on them and even the dark face grows brighter.

'When the just pray, they address divine goodness, and this sentiment of goodness drives away from them all shadows of fear. Serenity on the face of man is the radiating light of the divine countenance.

'When anger is stilled in the heart of man, he dreams of God's forgiveness; but it is man alone who pardons, for God is never angered.

'Adam is driven from earthly paradise by the anger and maliciousness of the head of shadow, but the face of light smiles on him ceaselessly from its celestial paradise.

'Eden, divided by four rivers, is a mystery of the head of shadow. Obscure symbols come from obscure thought, the dogmatic god is the father of mysterious allegories.

'The higher Eden has no divisions or exclusions: there are no poisoned apples in the garden of the supreme God.

'But only the father knows this Eden, he alone understands his love, pitiless for all eternity, for he is without weakness and without anger.'

II

'Let us continue mentally to draw the hieroglyphic head which symbolizes the father. What eyes shall we give him?

'Eyes other than mortal eyes, eyes without lids and lashes.

'For God never sleeps; his eyes are never closed.

'Is it not written: "The guardian of Israel neither slumbers nor sleeps"?

'It is also written: "The eyes of the Lord gaze without ceasing throughout the expanse of the universe."

'And yet it is said: "The gaze of the Lord falls on those who fear him, the eye of Adonai is fixed on Israel."

'Is this a contradiction? No, in truth. For the Lord who sees the entire universe is the god of light; he who sees and prefers a single people is the god of shadow.

'The preference accorded Israel would be an injustice and hence a lie, if God did not look at the same throughout the whole of the universe. The eye of privilege would see poorly if he were not sustained, rectified by the eye of justice. It is for this reason that we give two eyes to the supreme head; but these two eyes are the two ends of an ellipse, and this ellipse of two eyes makes only one eye in all.

'This single eye has three rays and three halos.

'These halos are crowns which constitute the triple kingdom of all things visible to God.

'There are two eyes, but should one wish to distinguish between them, they merge into one.

'This is the right eye of the single face composed of light and shadow, for the two faces are in fact one, as the two eyes are one eye.

'The left eye, this is the Microprosopopeia, and it has eyebrows which frown and eyelids which close.

'This one slumbers often, for it is made in the image of man, and it is this one we address when we say: "Lord, awake! and turn your eye upon us."

'Woe to the man who sees the eye of God as red, inflamed with anger!

'He who believes in a wrathful God, where will he seek his pardon?

'The Ancient of days is all goodness, and the beam of his eye is always the whitest and purest of lights.

'Happy is the lot of the just and wise man, who views all with this same purity and whiteness!

'It is written: "Come, family of Jacob, and walk in the light of Adonai."

'The name of the supreme master remains, however, shrouded in mystery.

'Nowhere in the law is it explained, except in this passage where God says to Abraham: "I swear by my own self that through you shall Israel be blessed."

'Who can so bind himself by an oath, if not the human God? And what is Israel in the divine order, if not the divine faith of Israel?

'And if God says through the mouth of the prophet: "Israel, you shall be my glory," is this not the God of shadow who wishes to glorify himself in the splendour of Israel's God of light?

'To give him a name, we call him the Ancient of days. As it is said in the prophecy of Daniel: "I have seen thrones overturned and the Ancient of days sit down."

'Stand up, Rabbi Jehuda, and tell us what are these thrones which are overturned.'

'It is written,' said Rabbi Jehuda: 'His throne is the seat of life-giving fire. God sits on the throne and fire gives life instead of devouring and destroying.

'If God leaves the throne, the fire is extinguished; otherwise whole worlds might be consumed.

'Where God is seated, there is balance.

'When his power makes for itself a centre, it creates a new universe, and all the others displace themselves to rotate around it. For God moves in order to seat himself, and he seats himself in order to move.'

And Rabbi Simeon said to Rabbi Jehuda: 'May God direct you in the eternal ways and may he remain in your thoughts.'

III

'Come and see. It is written: "I am, before all things, myself. In the beginning I am, and at the end of all I am myself, wholly."

'Everything is him, for everything reveals him. He hides within all that is. His breath gives life to all that breathes, and this is why, among the mysteries of his allegorical face, we shall now speak of the symbolism of the nose.

'It is the nose, above all, on which the character of a face depends.

'Now, the head of light and the head of shadow are of quite different characters.

'The nose of the supreme head breathes life toward the lower head.

'From one nostril comes personal life, from the other, collective life.

'But the unique spirit of this double breath is appeasement and pardon.

'It is this breath which, in the time of the Messiah, is to still all storms and quiet all angers.

'The spirit of wisdom and intelligence,

'The spirit of counsel and strength,

'The spirit of knowledge and awe of the Lord.

'Are these different spirits? We have said the breath of the father is single. Stand up, Rabbi José.'

Rabbi José got up and from his place said: 'In the days of the Messiah, wisdom will no longer be hidden, for understanding will flower.

'The breath of the father, the spirit of God will come with the six spirits that are in actuality one, like the six steps of Solomon's single throne.

'Thus are explained the seven spirits of the throne spoken of by the ancient prophets. These are the seven hues of light, the seven notes of music, the seven breathings which form the one breath of spirit.'

'May yours,' said Rabbi Simeon, 'rest in peace in the world to come!

'Come now and see: When the prophet Ezekiel invokes spirit to bring the dead back to life, he summons the four breaths which make up the spirit of life.

'What are these four quickening breaths? That of God towards man, that of man towards God, that which results from their mingling, and lastly, the immense and eternal breath of God which circles around all worlds and returns to the mouth of the father.

'These four breaths are in reality one: the spirit of life.

'Thus the prophet, turning to face the four cardinal points, summons only a single spirit.

'Is it not said that in the time of the Messiah's reign, when the spirit of understanding and knowledge shall be infused into all flesh, each human soul, without need of teaching, shall know the truth.

'For at that time, when the veils of falsehood will be forever torn asunder, souls will no longer be separated by error in all its forms and will live one through the other, looking freely one within another.

'Each will radiate and receive the light of all others, by a sort of universal inhalation and exhalation.

'Thus in all things is the spirit of life composed of four breaths.

'There will come a time of universal resurrection for the life of the intelligence.

'For these four spirits in one are symbolized by the square which encloses the triangle, and thus is explained, in the symbolism of numbers, the mystery of the seven spirits.

'The nose of the white-haired old one, the nose of the supreme head, breathes creations that are forever new. That of the head of shadow breathes destruction and consuming fire.

'The dark head breathes in life and exhales death; the white head takes in death and breathes out life.

'Who can conceive of these strange and monstrous heads? Who has ever seen them, and who will ever understand them?

'The kings of kings, that is, the masters of science and wisdom, can alone understand where and why the imagination draws their outlines and how it can be so that, at one and the same time, they do and do not exist.'

The Mysteries
of the White Beard

Rabbi Simeon had paused a moment; he took up again where he had left off, saying: 'Woe to him who reaches with profane hands towards the majestic beard of the father of fathers! For this beard is glorious beyond all glory, a mystery which enfolds all mysteries. No one has seen it, no one may touch it.

'The beard is the adornment of adornments, the majesty of majesties.

'The beard forms the link between the ears and mouth, it radiates from the lips like the word which gives light and life to the soul.

'It is for this reason that we take it as a symbol of the Word.

'It contains all mysteries and teaches all truths.

'It is white as snow and casts a shadow darker than night.

'It is divided into thirteen parts on which are poured the most precious of perfumes: the two parts descending from the nose to the corners of the mouth, separated by a scant space of flesh; the two parts which join the beard to the beginning of the ears; the beard itself, divided into three sections, each divided again into three.

'This beard is perfect, since we take it to be the Word, which is, itself, perfect.

'It is all beauty, all balance, all rightness.

'The cheeks shine forth from above, like two scarlet apples, projecting the light of life on to the sombre Microprosopopeia.

'White and red combined are the colour of the mysterious rose, the whiteness of milk and the redness of blood, the white of light and the redness of fire.

'All in nature that is white and red derives from the supreme rose.

'The thirteen parts of the white beard represent the synthesis of all truths, and the man who understands this allegorical beard is a man full of truth.

'Do we not say proverbially of a wise, strong man, of a man who lowers his eyes reflectively before undertaking an enterprise: This is a man who considers his beard!

'And those who raise a hand and swear on oath on the beard of the old man, these swear on the truth itself, symbolized by the thirteen sections of the supreme beard.

'Four, the four letters of the holy name, the four elements, the four corners of a square, the four cardinal points of heaven, and nine, that is, three multiplied by three: the active and the passive and the equilibrium they create as they reproduce themselves.'

Mystery of the Black Beard

Does the beard of the Microprosopopeia possess such a system and orderly disposition? Stand up, Rabbi Isaac, and speak to us of the parts of the black beard.'

Rabbi Isaac stood and began: 'Listen to these thirteen sayings of the prophet Micah:

I
Is there any who can be likened to you, Lord?

II
You take away injustice and cause it to disappear.

III
You pass, treading on sin.

IV
For it is your desire in the end, that your people be saved.

V
You will not for ever remain angry.

VI
For your wish is for forgiveness.

VII
Mercy will come to us again.

VIII
Our iniquities shall be vanquished.

IX

Even the last memory of our faults shall be buried in the very bottom of the sea.

X

To the family of Jacob shall be given the heritage of truth.

XI

And to the family of Abraham, eternal mercy.

XII

We trust in the oath which you gave to our fathers.

XIII

We believe in the promise made in olden times.

'These,' continued Rabbi Isaac, 'are thirteen drops of precious balm, fallen from the thirteen parts of the supreme beard, and which bring order to the chaos of the lower beard.

'The dark beard is made up of coarse, unwieldy hairs, tangled together.

'But the thirteen drops of the balm of mercy force them to adapt to the harmonious disposition of the higher beard.

'For the white beard sends down to the black its long, supple, silken strands, and its rivers of gentleness soften the coarseness of this dark fleece.

'Thick twisted hairs are often a mark of intellectual servitude.

'And if one considers the hair an extension of the brain, a quiet, lucid thought must be represented by a head of hair that is even, supple and soft.

'Now, the mouth is analogous to, yet distinct from, the hair. The hair takes up its growth behind the ears, and near the ears begins the beard which radiates outwards from the mouth.

'The black beard is the shadow of the white, as the law is the shadow of freedom, and as a threat is the shadow of forgiveness and love.

'Now, we have said that light and shadow are necessary to the manifestation of day, and that all illumination is perceived as a mixture of light and shade.

'Thus can we say that, in divine revelation, absolute shadow does not exist: all is light.

'The light which shines is the white light; and the light which envelops itself in shadow is the black light.

'The law is written on a white page with black coals, taken from the altar with tongs by the Seraphim.

'This is the great sheet of light, bearing characters of fire.

'It is for this reason we represent divine thought, the spirit of the scriptures, by a soft, white beard, in contrast to the other, both tangled and rough.

'For one is an image of spirit, the other, the letter of the law.

'The same can be said for the heads of hair. That of the God of light is as white as snow, its strands even and flowing.

'That of the God of shadow is as black as a raven's wing, and its locks are twisted and snarled.

'But the white beard impregnates the black beard with its perfumes, and the hair of the head of light permeates the hair of shadows with its splendour, so that the two heads of hair and the two beards belong to a sole identical head, which is the symbolic and allegorical image of God.

Details
Concerning the Great White Beard

Part One

The first part of the mysterious beard is that which begins near the right ear, descending to the corner of the mouth.

'The beard has its origin in the virile heat of the blood, thus we may call it the daughter of the heart of man; but here, since it more or less continues the hair, itself a radiation of the brain, we may also call it the daughter of thought.

'The hairs are tender, soft, they have attained no great length. This is the Word in divine generation.

'There are thirty-one small curls, arranged in perfect order, and each curl is made up of three hundred and ninety hairs.

'These numbers represent worlds of intellect which God wishes to bring into being by means of the Word. Each world is to engender other worlds, multiplied by the mysterious figure, two, and the holy figure, three.

'From tens to hundreds, from hundreds to myriads, worlds are multiplied by reason of creative ideas, in exact proportion to the germinal origins already formed.

'Each hair of the young-growing beard ends in a point of light, and each point of light works to produce a sun.

'For each sun there comes into being a night, which this new star will enliven, a night filled with phantoms and horrors that the nascent sun illumines and dissipates with a smile.

'It is thus that the glowing beard of the father streams out toward the rough, black beard of the God of darkness.

'And one cannot perceive the supreme beard, except in the brilliance it gives to the beard of shadow.

'Is it not said in the book of Psalms: "The perfume of the supreme head is poured out on to the beard of the father, and from there, on to the beard of Aaron"?

'What is Aaron? He is the great priest. And what is the great priest, if not the shadow and human personification of the dark God?

'The psalm we have quoted begins by saying that the perfection of good and the triumph of happiness lies in the remaining together of brothers.

'Who are these brothers, if not the two old ones?

'For us, God has need of a high priest, but this high priest would become the night of death, were he to be separated from God.

'God gives his light to the priest, and the priest lends to God his shadow.

'The priest is the brother of God, as shadow is the sister of light.

'What the priest does on earth in the exercise of his ministry, God performs in heaven, with a difference as that of right to left, of day to night, of reproachful anger to peace-giving mercy.

'And it is thus that religious harmony results from the analogy of opposites.'

'May supreme harmony shine down on you!' said Rabbi Simeon to Rabbi Isaac. 'May the glowing beard be the sign of your eternal strength! May we together see the face of the Ancient of days, and may the peace and joy of righteous souls be your lot and mine in the world to come!'

Part Two

Stand, Rabbi Chiskija, and from where you are tell us the glories of one part of the holy beard.'

Rabbi Chiskija got up and said:

'It is written: "I am my beloved's, and his good will is turned toward me."

'It is for man, for each one of us, that the supreme thought becomes the Word, the creator of all thoughts and all substance.

'I see a river of light, descending from divine understanding and changing into three hundred and thirty-five harmonious voices.

'In this light, night comes to bathe, cleansing itself of shadow.

'I saw shadowy forms plunge deep in the white waves, coming out again as white as the waves themselves.

'And I prayed the higher intelligences to explain to me what I had seen.

'And I was answered: "You see in what manner injustice is effaced by God.

' "For between his ear and his mouth, between his understanding and his Word, there is no place for falsehood.

' "In the living light, in the light which reaches everywhere, shadow cannot exist; and should it wish to, it must necessarily take on a whiteness, transforming itself to light.

' "Now, it is thus that God will one day change man's evil into good."

'This is what I am inspired to say by the second part of the holy beard, analogous and parallel to the first.'

Rabbi Chiskija, having so spoken, regained his seat.

Rabbi Simeon said then: 'The world is no longer for us an enigma nor a hell. Be blessed, oh Rabbi Chiskija, by the supreme old one, for you have consoled our hearts.

'All the rays converge towards their centre: I see the harmonious totality of the Creator's work. From the heights we occupy we can already see the holy land in the impending flowering of its destiny.

'We can see that which Moses himself was denied when he went up a second time into Mount Sinai: the sun of justice in which we believe, the sun which is to come, illuminating our faces.

'I feel mine glowing with faith and hope, and more fortunate than Moses, I know why it is so. Moses did not even know that his face had grown luminous through contemplation of God.

'I see before my eyes this allegorical beard, as if it had been sculpted by a capable hand in thirteen parts, representing the whole of truth.

'As you explain them, I see all these parts arrange themselves in orderly fashion, firmly attached to the ideal head which supports the mysterious crown.

'The king appears to me, then, as if from a mid-point in his uncountable years. Effects come together with causes, causes are united, set forth by principles, and the principle of principles reigns with sovereign dominion from its centre which is everywhere.

'Rejoice, my companions, in this holy revelation, for the world surely will not understand what we have been given to understand, nor see what we can now see, before the Messiah's reign!'

The Other Parts

Thus, one by one, the great rabbis analysed the holy beard. Explanation must now be given directly, summarizing, as it were, the vague subtlety and lengthiness of their exact words.

The hair, radiating outwards from the skull, is for these great priests an image of divine thought; likewise is the beard, radiating outwards from the mouth, a symbol of the holy word. The hair is the Word of God in its own awareness of itself; the beard is the Word made manifest, in works or in inspired writings. This beard is divided into thirteen parts because the secret theology of the Qabalists is inextricably bound to the nine ciphers which make up all numbers and to the four letters which make up the name of Jehovah.

The science of numbers, taken as the algebra of ideas, is the Beraschith; the science of the letters of the sacred name is the Mercavah. Beraschith or Bereschith means genesis, generation or geneology. Mercavah means chariot, as if the four symbolic letters were the wheels of God's chariot which Ezekiel saw in a vision. These were wheels of light, turning one in another, celestial spheres, intersecting circles whose centres are everywhere, whose circumferences are everywhere, whose common centre is everywhere, and whose final, definitive circumference is nowhere.

But the name of Jehovah has in reality only three letters, since the fourth is a repetition of the second: *Jod-Hé-Van-Hé.*

Thus the thirteen sections of the supreme beard are the equivalent of the cycle of twelve, plus the centre which must be given to these numbers in order to arrange them in a circle on the clock of time.

These theological subtleties linked to numerical abstractions were, so to speak, the scholastic system of the ancient rabbis, fathers of Qabalistic philosophy. The result of this method was deductions which, often sublime, sometimes puerile, were nevertheless exact. 'God,' said Solomon, 'created everything with weight, measure and number.' It was the natural conclusion in the thought of certain naive thinkers that algebra was the sacred fire of Prometheus and that men could be created by pronouncing words. This is sometimes true, as great orators know so well, but only in a metaphorical, figurative sense. Doubtless matter obeys the movement resulting from forces which can be determined by numbers. For the Hebrews, numbers are symbolized by the letters of the alphabet, and thus it was by means of these letters that God created space and worlds. The letter is, in fact, the conventional sign of power, but a sign only, not power itself. In similar fashion, in the book of the Sohar which we are examining, the great rabbis assembled round Rabbi Simeon attach their ideas on divinity to the allegorical figure of a human head, whose eyes and ears represent understanding, whose hair represents thought, whose beard represents the word, or rather, the expression and manifestation of truth. They have said repeatedly that this head has no existence in visible or tangible reality, that God is inaccessible to our senses and even to our thought, that we can understand him only through his action upon us and relative to us. All of which has not kept a great number of superstitious men from attributing a human visage to God, and not only in far-off times, but recently as well.

Swedenborg, for example, this otherwise astonishing and admirable mystic, maintains that the universe is in reality an immense man with hair of light, with legs and arms of stars, truly made in the image of God, who is himself so great and so brilliant a man that no human eye can see him. The Mormons, in these very days in which we live, believe that the universe is limited and that God, in the form of a gigantic man, occupies the centre, seated on a colossal Urim-Thummim, that is, on two great precious stones with innumerable facets in which are reflected all that comes to pass in the existing worlds. This thought is scarcely more advanced than that of the Scandinavians in which Odin is seated beneath an oak along whose branches there scampers eternally a squirrel who comes to whisper in his ear all that happens in the universe.

Let us pass over the details of the thirteen sections of the allegorical beard so as not to tire our readers, examining only the conclusions which Rabbi Simeon draws from them.

Conclusion
Concerning
the Allegorical Figure of the Macroprosopopeia

Then said Rabbi Simeon to his companions: 'Your words are like embroidery on the great veil which permits us, without being dazed and blinded, to lift our eyes towards the eternal light.

'I saw this work being done as you spoke: your thoughts determined the image, and the image came of itself to take its place in this wondrous tapestry.

'It was thus that in former times Moses had the holy tabernacle's veil embroidered and hung from four columns by rings of gold.

'Thus the sacrificial altar had four corners, like the square that can be drawn in all the circles of the heavens;

and there was in the middle of the altar a hooked bar which served to stir the sacrificial fire, for this fire could not be touched by human hands.

'Our allegories are like this bar, allowing us to touch the burning truth. We progress, with well-ordered imagination, thanks to the law of analogies and the exactness of numbers. What we know serves as a basis for what we believe. The order which we see calls for the order we suppose exists in the heights beyond our comprehension. Thus, nothing in our images is left to chance, all is fixed in a harmonious and justifiable order. You speak and the picture takes shape. Your voice determines the forms which appear, and they arrange themselves in all magnificence, like the ornaments of a crown.

'The columns of the temple are moved: they seem reborn, emerging from the ground to hear you.

'The armies of heaven surround you, and their admirable discipline justifies your words.

'Oh! be happy in the world to come, for the words which come out of your mouth are fore-ordained by truth and justice, following the path of righteousness without fail, straying neither to the right nor to the left.

'The most holy God, whom you bless, rejoices to hear them, and he listens to them that they may be accomplished.

'For, in the world to come, all good words spoken in the world at hand will take on living forms, and you are creatures of goodness, you who manifest through the Word that which is true!

'The truth is a fine wine which never vanishes. It falls drop by drop from the cup of the wise, reaching even beyond the grave to moisten the lips of the dead. It descends even to the hearts of our sleeping fathers, making them speak again, as in a dream.

'For the truth is always alive, it abandons no one once it has touched him.

'And when the children on earth give living testimony to

it, the fathers who sleep beneath the earth begin to smile, answering softly: "Amen!" '

The Microprosopopeia

We know of nothing in the ancient books as great as this great council of initiates, busying themselves, in truth and reason, with the creation of a hieroglyphic figure of God. They know that any form, in order to be seen, must have light and cast a shadow. But can shadow represent supreme intelligence? No, of course not. It can only represent its veil. The ancient Isis was veiled; Moses, speaking of God, covered his head with a veil. All theology of the ancients is veiled with more or less transparent allegories: mythology is nothing other than this. To mythology there succeeded the mysteries, which are the darkened veil, stripped of its adornments, pointing more and more to the face of shadow outlined by the great Rabbi Simeon. But all this harkens back to the first, the earliest imagery, so that the pages we translate here, by analysing them, seem to be the origin of all symbolisms and the fundamental principle of all dogmas.

Nothing is as beautiful nor as encouraging as this explanation given to certain images of the Bible, representing God as wrathful, repentant or changeable, in the manner of man. Such emotional behaviour, Simeon Ben-Jochai would say, belongs only to the face of shadow: it is the mirror of human passion. The face of light is always peaceful and radiant, but God, who has no face, remains unchanging above this light and shadow. The man who seeks God can find only man's ideal; how can the finite conceive of the infinite?

Ordinary man must have a God which resembles himself. If the master did not grow angry when men do evil, they would believe that evil goes unpunished, and thus would remain unchecked in their wickedness. If the

master were not harsh, severe, mysterious, difficult to
satisfy and to understand, they would easily fall prey to
indifference and indolence. Troublesome childhood has
need of the rod, and the father must know how to feign
anger, even though he may wish to smile at the mischiev-
ousness of his children.

Thus, according to our ancient masters, the image of
divinity has two faces, one which surveys the faults of man
and becomes angry, the other which contemplates eternal
justice and smiles.

This mystery of higher initiation was known even to the
Greeks, who sometimes gave to Pluto the attributes of
Jupiter. Egypt prayed to the black Serapis, and images of
Bacchus have been preserved wherein this god whose
adventures recall the story of Moses, this god whose
celebrations brought forth the cry *Io Evohé (Jod hé Van
hé)*, the four letters of Jehovah's name, is shown like Janus
with two faces. One is young and fair like that of Apollo,
the other, grotesque and frowning like that of Silenus.

Apollo and Bacchus characterize the two principles of
exaltation in mankind: enthusiasm and drunkenness. Sublime souls find intoxication in poetry and beauty, vulgar
souls seek enthusiasm in the drunkenness that wine
produces.

But for the vulgar man, wine is not the only source of
exaltation. Lowly men grow drunk on all 'vapours' which
affect the brain: insatiable greed, undisciplined lusts, vain
glory, fanaticism. There exist ascetic imaginations even
wilder and madder than those of the Bacchantes; there are
self-styled protectors of the faith who, changing sweetness
to bitterness and true preaching to satire, are condemned
by incorruptible nature to wear the satyr's mask. Insol-
ence, like red-hot iron, has burned their lips, and their
guarded eyes denounce, in spite of them, the perversity of
their hearts.

The face of shadow which our rabbis describe is not,
however, the God of Garasse, of Patouillet or Veuillot; it is

the veiled god of Moses, the after-God, if I may refer to
him thus, thereby alluding to a Biblical allegory. Moses
prayed to God, to the invisible God, to appear. 'Look in
the cleft of this rock,' said the Lord. 'I will pass and lay
my hand thereon, and when I will have passed, you shall
see me from behind.'

Moses, writing this page, was conscious of the symbolism of the head of shadow, the only one which it is given
to man to look upon without being blinded by light. The
God of light is he of whom the wise man dreams; the God
of shadow is the dream of the foolish. Human folly sees
everything in reverse, and if we may use the daring
metaphor of Moses, the face which the multitudes worship
is only the divine image glimpsed from behind, the
after-shadow of God. 'Videbis posteriora mea.'

The Text of the Sohar Continued
Prologue concerning the Microprosopopeia

Ready yourselves now, and give your attention to a
symbolic description of the Microprosopopeia, this veil of
shadow fitted to cover a shape of light, this visible fiction
which makes the splendour of the invisible accessible to
our eyes, the dark old one who gathers in and reflects the
light of the white old one.

'Wisdom is your guide, your tools are order, justice and
beauty.

'Give a form to the whole body of human thought
which ascends toward the invisible author of all forms.

'And let this form be a human one, for we seek the king
who shall reign over all men.

'A human form, so that we can seat it on a throne and
worship it.

'Has not the prophet said: "I saw a throne in the
heavens, and on this throne some immense thing resem-
bling a human form"?

'Let us use the human form, for this is for us the synthesis of all forms.

'For the name of man is for us the synthesis of all names.

'Let us use the human form, for the human idea contains for us all the secrets of thought, and all the mysteries of the ancient world, the world created before man, the world in which no balance could be attained until the appearance of the form called Adam.'

The Kings of Edom

'We read in the book of Mystery: "Before the Ancient of ancients revealed his grandeur, he let there come into being gigantic forces which, before the advent of the people of God, reigned like kings in the land of Edom."

'Nature was given over to the spirit of their enmity, and they eventually destroyed each other. For they could not reach an agreement as to how to form a human body, seeing as how they, themselves, lacked a head.

'The human head was missing from all living nature, and nature was in a state of chaos, like the human mind when it lacks the idea of God!

'Thus these terrestrial Elohims, these anarchic kings of the world, were destroyed.

'They were destroyed, but they were not annihilated.

'Destroyed as reckless powers, they were preserved as powers which must be controlled.

'And they took their place in the order of things, when order was created.

'As a matter of fact, nothing is ever destroyed, everything simply changes place, shifts position, and when beings change in obedience to the eternal order, it is this which we, as men, call dying.

'Even the king of Egypt is not dead, he has come down from his throne to make place for the Eternal.

'It is said that Adam named all beings, for at the time of his coming a hierarchy instigated itself in nature, and all beings, finding themselves for the first time in their appointed place, had just reason to be called and determined by a name.

'Only one of the pre-Adamite monsters was not destroyed, the great Androgyn, male and female like the palm tree.

'This is the productive, generative force which existed before Adam and which God will not destroy.

'It existed, but it was not controlled; it was at work, but the law of its working was not fixed until it had produced its master work: the living form of Adam.'

The Skull of the Microprosopopeia

(Air, Fire and Dew)

'When the white head decided to add to its beauty with an ornament, it sent out a spark from its own light.

'It breathed on the spark to cool it, and the spark grew firm.

'It expanded and hollowed itself out, like a blue, transparent skull enclosing thousands, myriads of worlds.

'This cavity is full of eternal dew, white on the side of the father, red on the side of the son. It is the dew of light and life, the dew that engenders universes and resurrects the dead.

'Some are resurrected in light, and the others in fire.

'Some in the eternal whiteness of peace, the others in the redness of fire and the torments of war.

'The wicked are the disgrace, so to speak, of their father, and it is they who cover the face with its redness.

'In this skull of universal man, only begotten son of God, resides knowledge, with its thirty-two paths and its fifty gates.'

The Hair of the Microprosopopeia

'Hair represents thoughts, as it radiates outward from the head.

'The head of the Microprosopopeia is surrounded by myriads of myriads and millions of millions of black hairs, coarse and kinked and tangled together.

'There, intermingled, are to be found the bright and the dark, the true and the false, the just and the unjust.

'These hairs are divided in the centre by a single straight line, corresponding identically to one on the white head.

'For balance is the same for God and for man, and the laws which govern balance are no different in heaven than on earth.

'Among human thoughts, some are harsh and pitiless, others are soft and pliable.

'The same sense of balance weighs them and modifies the rigidity of the left by the mercifulness of the right.'

The Forehead of the Microprosopopeia

(The Eyes and their Colour)

'When the forehead of light, is shining, the forehead of shadow is bathed in its glow.

'When anger brings shadows to cover the forehead of the God of man, the dark twisted hairs stand on end, a breath of ire makes them hiss like serpents.

'Prayers of ignorance rise like a black smoke and cloud the forehead of the idol still more.

'Then rises the prayer of the just.

'It comes out of the shadow and ascends directly towards the light.

'The celestial head bends down, and the shadowy forehead below is bathed in splendours.

'Ire ceases, the storm abates and vengeance is changed to forgiveness.'

The Eyes

'He has black, thick eyebrows; round his eyes bristle lashes the colour of shadow.

'When his sombre eyelids open, he seems then to awaken.

'His gaze takes on the reflection of the higher light and resembles the gaze of God.

'It is to him the prophet speaks when he says: "Awake, Lord, why do you sleep so long? Is it not time to shake off your sleep at last?"

'During the sleep of the God of shadow, foreign nations gain dominion over Israel.

'The God of man slumbers when man's faith falls asleep.

'But when our God wakes, he rolls his eyes and, casting a scornful glance at the nations which oppress us, he overwhelms them with his lightning.

'When they are open, his eyes are soft like the eyes of doves, and there are to be found these basic colours, black, white, yellow, red.

'The black of the Microprosopopeia's eyes can be linked to that stone which comes forth from the abyss once every thousand years, from the abyss of the great sea.

'And when this stone appears, a great tempest arises, the waves are lashed into fury, and the noise they make is heard by the immense serpent, named Leviathan.

'This stone comes from the deep abyss, it rolls in the boiling torment of the sea, out of which it rises at last; and darkness covers all, a darkness next to which all other darknesses seem as nothing. Now, the initiated know that in this darkness are hidden all the mysteries of knowledge.

'Such is the darkness of the eye of the old one, a blackness containing and surpassing all obscurity.

'His whiteness is borrowed from the supreme gaze: it is the milk of mercy, falling upon him drop by drop like tears.

'His redness is that of fire, which destroys and renews life.

'His look of kindness is burnished yellow, shining like gold.

'When he grows wrathful, when he threatens, in the corners of his flashing eyes there hang two tears.

'His lightning bursts forth, his anger plunges to the depths of the abyss, fire breaks out, devouring its victims for ever.

'The powerful of the earth are overthrown, cedars are twisted like blades of grass, the abyss is gratified, anger is appeased, the sombre God grows calm, and on the hanging tears glows a brilliant beam from the light of a God of love.

'The eyelids close, the tears fall, and in falling they extinguish the fire of eternal hell.'

The Nose and the Beard
Analysis

Simeon Ben-Jochai continued to explain the Book of Mystery, describing the anatomy of the dark God. This God is neither the Ahriman of the Persians, nor the evil principle of the Manicheans: this is a loftier concept, a mediating shade between infinite light and the feeble eye of man, a veil, made in humanity's image, with which God deigns to veil his glory. In this shadow, the meaning of all mysteries is to be found. This shadow explains the terrible God of the prophets, the God who threatens and calls for fear. It is the God of priests, the God who requires sacrifice, the God who slumbers and wakes to the sound of trumpets from the temple, the God who repents of having created man, and who, won over by prayers and offerings, is appeased as he raises his hand to strike.

It must be remarked here that this obscure conception of divinity, far from seeming a poor one to the great rabbis and revelators of mystery, appears, rather, just and essential.

The ancient sanctuary was veiled, and when the veil was torn, this catastrophe heralded the end of a religion and of a world. The veil is not torn without the earth trembling: this happened at the death of Christ; but the sanctuary unveiled is a sanctuary profaned. Soon Caligula will place his idols there, waiting for the torches fired by Titus's soldiers. A voice cries; the gods have taken leave, while Christianity silently prepares another sanctuary and weaves another veil.

The two figurative heads of the old ones must be represented as concentric or superimposed in such a way that one is the reflection of the other, but a reflection in opposition, the white in the one being black in the other and vice versa.

The great rabbis apply themselves diligently to detailing the two heads, they count the tresses of hair and the divisions of the beard, they describe the two noses and the contrary streams of breath escaping from the four nostrils. The long and majestic nose of the supreme father breathes divine and eternal life; the short, wrinkled nose of the irate God breathes fire and smoke: this is the smouldering volcano of earthly life as well as what the great rabbis seem to mean by the eternal fire of hell.

This fire, say they, can be quenched only by the altar's fire, and this smoke dispelled only by the smoke of sacrifice. He can be understood, this dark God with the smouldering nostrils, for ever inflamed for they are the very vents of hell.

Here the dark God takes on something of our Devil, and it is to this particular fiction of the rabbis that the Persian Ahriman, the wicked God of the Manicheans, and the Christian Devil, all owe their common origin. It is a disfigured symbol: no longer the shadow of God, but, so to speak, a distorted mask, a caricature of the shadow. This misrepresentation, produced by ignorance working on so bold an image, proves the necessity for occultism and justifies the secrecy of the rabbis in shrouding the Qabalah in mystery.

After the nose, the rabbi describes the ears of the dark God. They are covered with wiry hairs, for in man, of whom the dark God is the image, understanding is clouded by the disorder of thought. When the vulgar God slumbers, his ears do not hear and evil is done in the world. The evil which offends and angers the God of shadow does not exist for the God of light. Relative to absolute order, disorder does not exist.

When the God of men awakens, he shakes out his hair, and the sky trembles. Then his ears are uncovered and available for prayer. These are days of victory for Israel: they triumph over Aman and vanquish their enemies.

From the ears, Rabbi Simeon passes to the beard, describing its separate sections. He counts nine of them, not thirteen as in the white beard of the supreme old one, because the negative Word of the God of shadow could never explain the divine quaternary. The ternary multiplied by itself gives nine, and this is the number for every hierarchy and classification in the Qabalistic method. There are nine choirs of angels; there are also nine classes of demons. The number nine has, then, its luminous and shadowy sides, but the divine quaternary is the perfect number which admits no negation. The negation of the quaternary would be the monstrous fiction of absolute evil. This would be the Satan of the diabolists, an impossible monster, unknown to the ancient masters, the great Hebrew Qabalists.

The nine sections of the beard of shadow represent the negative Word. These are the shadows of the great lights.

The great lights are the nine divine conceptions which precede the idea of creation.

First Light
The crown or supreme power

Shadow of this light
Despotism or absolute power

Second Light
Eternal wisdom
Shadow of this light
Blind faith

Third Light
Active intelligence
Shadow of this light
The dogma which claims to be unchanging and
which inevitably develops

Fourth Light
Spiritual beauty
Shadow of this light
Blind faith

Fifth Light
Eternal justice
Shadow of this light
Divine vengeance

Sixth Light
Infinite mercy
Shadow of this light
Voluntary sacrifice

Seventh Light
The eternal victory of good
Shadow of this light
Abnegation and voluntary austerity

Eighth Light
Eternity of goodness

Shadow of this light
Everlasting hell

Ninth Light
Fertility of goodness
Shadow of this light
Celibacy and sterility

Here, necessarily, the dark numbers stop, for the
number ten is the number of creation. But creation cannot
be negative. Celibacy and sterility produce nothing.

Celibacy has always been mysticism's dream, even in
Judaism which formally condemns sterility.

Asceticism is in fact incompatible with the duties of the
family. Travelling prophets had no wives. The family is the
world, and mysticism is the desert.

The family is true life, and mysticism is dreaming.

The family necessitates property, and mysticism commands abnegation and voluntary austerity.

Mysticism is the religious sentiment pushed to the
extreme. Thus, should it be tempered and governed by
sacerdotal authority; mystics are children whose peda-
gogues and tutors are the priests. We speak here of
orthodox mystics who escape the drunkenness of folly
thanks to the limitations of obedience. Undisciplined
mystics are madmen capable of great fury and which it
would be wise to shut away.

The Microprosopopeia
Considered as Androgynous

Here is what we have learned:

Rabbi Simeon then said: 'These mysteries of the Word
should be revealed only to those who can maintain
equilibrium with one foot on each end of the scale. They
must not be told to those who have not entered the crypt

of great trials, but only to those who have entered there and come out again.

'For he who enters but does not come out again, it would be better were he never to have been created.'

Commentary

Here we can clearly see that the occult dogma of Moses, professed to by Rabbi Simeon, comes from the sanctuaries of Egypt. There, in fact, one was subjected to great trial before being admitted to initiation. These trials took place in immense underground spaces, which those who gave way to fear were never to leave. The adept who, on the contrary, came out again triumphant, received the key to all religious mysteries, and the first great revelation, whispered close to his ear in passing, was contained in this formula:

Osiris is a dark God

That is: the God worshipped by the profane is only a shadow of the true God.

We give him man's anger so that he may be dreaded by man.

For if men are not presented with a master who resembles them, the idea of divinity will so surpass their feeble intelligence that it will escape them completely, and they will fall into atheism.

When man does evil, he throws himself into disorder, he transgresses the law which guards his happiness. Then he is miserable, dissatisfied with himself, and he is told that God is angry with him, in order to explain to him the workings of his own angered conscience. He must placate God with expiations which, like punishments inflicted on unreasonable, wilful children, serve to impress on the mind a horror of evil. He must above all return to the path of goodness, and then, from the calm he experiences, he feels that God has forgiven him. God, however, does not forgive, for he is never angered; but if you say to the vulgar man that the supreme judge lives in the heart of his own conscience, he will believe that God is only a word, and he will come to argue with his conscience, attributing his scruples or his remorse to learned prejudice. He will thus have no other guide than the self-interest of his passions which are the harbingers of death.

CONTINUATION OF THE TEXT

'Here is a summary of all these words:

'The Ancient of ancients exists within the Micropros-opopeia, light is hidden within shadow, the large is figured in the small: everything is in supreme unity. It is here that all has been, is and will be. Supreme unity will not change, has not changed, does not change.

'It has no forms, but conforms to our own. It takes on for us the form which contains all forms and the name which holds within it all names.

'This form, by means of which it can appear to us in our thoughts, is not really its form, it is the analogy of a form. It is an artificial head on which to place diadems and crowns.

'Man's form summarizes all forms, of higher as well as lower things.

'And because this form summarizes and represents all that is, we use it to make for ourselves a representation of God in the form of the supreme old one.

'Then, parallel to this form and as its shadow, our imagination creates the Microprosopopeia.

'And if you ask me what difference there is between the two old ones, I will answer that the two represent a single, selfsame thought.

'They are the two sides of an image: turned towards the sky, the image is serene and splendid; turned towards the ignorance and vice of man, the image is threatening and cloudy.

'Thus the Lord, during the exodus from Egypt, precedes

Israel in a cloud, luminous from Israel's side, but shadowy on the side of the Egyptians.

'Light and shadow, are they not opposed?

'They seem irreconcilable, contrary to such a degree that when one exists, the other cannot.

'They coincide admirably, however, and it is their harmonious accord which makes all forms visible.

'But these mysteries are accessible only to the harvesters of the sacred fields.

'It is written: "The mystery of the Lord belongs to those who fear him." '

Commentary

Here Rabbi Simeon attempts to explain the mysteries of Genesis where God is represented in human form creating Adam in his own image. This human form ascribed to God is the prototypal form of the great Adam, that is, of humanity in its entirety, pre-existing in the Word of God.

Now, by the great Adam whom they call Adam Kadmon or Adam the Protoplast, the Jewish initiates do not mean, as we do, the first human individual, but rather, have the entire human race appearing at once on the face of the earth. By the great Adam, they mean primitive humanity and even something more, for the body of Adam contains all animated beings and all the spirits of the universe. Thus they give to him the most gigantic proportions. His forehead touches the sun's zenith, his right hand touches the east, his left, the west. When he lifts his foot to walk, the shadow of his heel causes an eclipse of the sun. He is androgynous, with two faces, the masculine face in front, the feminine face behind. Each face is also androgynous, that is, masculine on the right and feminine on the left. The prototype of the great Adam which is in the Microprosopopeia is likewise androgynous in front, behind, to the right, to the left, on top and underneath, all of which symbolizes the universal equilibrium and balance of forces, either active or passive, in the whole of nature.

Symbols will make all of this more easily understood, and we can give several here.

We will not follow Rabbi Simeon in his descriptions of the divine androgyn contained in the prototype which is the dark old one or the God of shadow. These are monstrous anatomical fictions which recall the bizarre combinations of certain hybrid gods of India. A great thought presides over all these dream images, no doubt, but their expression is too far removed from our habits and modes of thinking. Suffice it to say that the rabbi represents typical couples, the Microprosopopeia with nature, his wife, and Adam Kadmon together with his Eve, in the act of eternal fertility, explaining their ardours and their amorous languor, making of immensity an enormous nuptial bed without alcove, covering or curtain.

On Justice
Following the Text of Rabbi Simeon

'Woman does not possess within herself strength and justice, these she must receive from man.

'She aspires after them with untellable thirst, but cannot receive them until she is entirely submissive.

'When she rules, she brings about only revolt and violence.

'It is in this way that woman became man's overseer by drawing him into sin.

'In the incontinence of her desires, she became a mother and gave birth to Cain.

'Then she said: "God and I have made a man, and this man is my property."

'She was not yet ready for true maternity, for the serpent had infected her with his jealousy and anger.

'The birth of the cruel and pitiless Cain was a violent and terrible one, exhausting all the energies of woman.

'She grew softer then, weaker, and brought forth the gentle Abel.

'These two conflicting generations could not find peace together: the strong, without measure, was destined to absorb the weak, without defence; and this is what occurred.

'Then the God of shadow awoke and he tore from the stomach of Cain this latter's brother whom he had devoured.

'But neither Cain nor Abel were considered just enough to remain alive before him.

'He relegated Abel to life's limbo regions and threw Cain into the great ocean of tears.

'There, they seek each other still in order to continue their struggle and each, on his own, produces a spirit of violence and weakness.

'Happy are the souls who descend in a direct line from the great Adam! For the children of the useless Abel and those of the criminal Cain are no better one than the other: they are the unjust, the sinners.

'True justice unites goodness and strength, it is neither violent nor weak.

'Happy are you, you who understand these words, words of the spirit which joins the right with the left, the higher with the lower.

'Happy are you, you the masters of masters, harvesters of the holy field, who contemplate and recognize the Lord, looking at him face to face, and who, by your union with the eternal Word, make yourselves worthy of immortality in the world to come.

'About you it is written: "From this day forth you will know that the Lord reigns at one time from the highest heaven and from the deepest earth."

'The Lord, the Ancient of days, God!, that is, the unique, the only, his reign is everywhere. May his name be blessed in this century and in the century of centuries!'

Final Words
On the Supreme Man

Rabbi Simeon said: 'By looking down on things, we see them from above, and by observing them from above, we see things which lie below.

'The ten fingers of our hands recall the ten crowns of knowledge, the holy numbers and their equilibrium, five on one side and five on the other.

'It is the same with our toes: that which is above is like that which is below.

'The higher forms govern the lower forms, the top is like the bottom, woman is analogous to man.

'Opposites govern opposites, extremes find contact, and different forms adhere one to another and act one upon another.

'Man and woman united together form the perfect body of humanity.

'They come one out of the other, they need one another, they act and react one on the other.

'The life they possess is the same: thus the blood in the body's vessels is distributed to the right and left throughout the entire body.

'All the vessels of the body intermingle their flow; all the nerves share in the communication of luminous fluid and sensitivity.

'Like worlds in space, sending each other again and again the light of their suns.

'All that is outside this mutual, universal life of the great body is foul. Do not go near spirits who exist outside the great communion, as if they might teach you something, for you will receive nothing from them but stain and blemish.

'These wandering spirits are like decapitated heads, forever thirsty, but the water they drink drips away with their blood and does not quench their thirst.'

'If it is thus, you say, the very angels are part of the great body of the Synagogue?'

'How could you doubt it?

'If it were not so, they could participate neither in holiness nor in life.

'For the synagogue of the wise is the body of humanity, the body of God.

'The angel of the Lord in the prophecy of Daniel, is he not called Gabriel? And what does Gabriel signify if not man *par excellence*, the man of God, or the Man-God?

'Tradition teaches us that vile spirits cannot take on the beauties of the human form, for they exist separately from the harmony of the perfect body.

'They are wanderers, flitting here and there throughout the world, unable to assume specific shape.

'They find themselves rejected everywhere, for they have in them the disobedience of Cain: they are driven from the field whose brilliant tents are the stars.

'Never can they take their stand within the realm of truth; at one moment they will hover above it, at another, below, but either way, they are always vile.

'The impure spirits coming from Abel are gentler and can approach the great body, even, to all appearances, attaching themselves to it.

'But they are as superfluous, artificial limbs: they are added to the body, but cannot remain there.

'All these spirits are like aborted beings or detached limbs floating in space: they listen from the heights or from the depths to all they can hear, but they understand nothing, as we all know who busy ourselves with the subject.

Translator's note:
Here the great master of the Qabalah seems to admit the existence of wandering spirits, scattered throughout the atmosphere, vague spirits as yet without particular form, a kind of impure larvae that the centre of life always relegates to the outer shadowy realm. Other Qabalists, supported in this by words of Jesus Christ himself, give us to believe that this outer shadowy kingdom is Gehenna or Hell, but

that it is impossible for any soul to stop and remain there. In these shadows, impure souls wither, totally spent, and after a more or less lengthy time of suffering are reduced to the first simplicity of their vital principle and having lost all memory, are once again attracted towards the realm of life. (See *Pneumatica Kabbalistica* and Issac de Soria's *De revolutionibus animarum*)

'Now, here is the tradition concerning the book's mystery. When the conjugal prototype regained its equilibrium through the appeasement of the God of shadow, the Adamic couple came together for the third time.

'And a balanced generation was made.

'Harmony was then established between heaven and earth.

'The higher world brought life to the lower, for man, the mediator between thought and form, had at last found peace.

'There was then the divine glory of the upper regions and the divine glory of the lower, the Shekinah of heaven and the Shekinah of earth.

'Holy is the Lord in the thoughts of heaven, holy is the Lord in the forms of earth, holy is the Lord whose thought descends from idea to form and back again!

'Holy, holy, holy is the Lord, the God of hosts, the God of harmonious beings, well ordered like armies!

'All the earth is full of his glory, and all that exists is a single body, given life by a single soul.

'Here is one of our traditions:

'There exists a compensatory balancing of beings one with another.

'It is written in the Song of Songs: "We will make for you gold necklaces inlaid with silver."

'It is thus that, to embellish one with the other, mercy and justice are united.

'And they are like the palm tree which always grows in twos; they are like brother and sister, ageing equally.

'Thus we know that he who separates himself from humanity by refusing to love, espousing no one, he will find no place after death in the great human synthesis, but

will remain outside, a stranger to the laws of attraction and
to the transformations of life.

'And nature, ashamed of him, will cause him to
disappear, as we hasten to rid ourselves of the dead.

'Why does the law command that, upon his death, we
do not leave the body of a man to pass the night in the
house in which he lived?

'It is out of respect for the human form, become useless,
that it may not be dishonoured.

'It is to prevent that which was once a person from
becoming a futile, nameless thing.

'It is to distinguish the venerable body of man from
animal carrion.

'Death must not be allowed authority when it is a question
of man: for man is the scope of immortal spirit.

'A human body without soul is a gap in nature, and yet
the corpse is worthy of honour because of its human
shape.

'One must make haste to put an end to this contradiction and it is for this reason that we bury our dead before
the night following their passing.

'Men who renounce their humanity in the hope of
conquering heaven are nothing more than dwarves who
wish to bring back the crimes of the giants, unrighteous,
contrary creatures.

'For it is written: "The sons of God, having seen the
daughters of man and finding them beautiful, bent down
too far to see them and were hurled into the abyss."

'There they engendered impure spirits and demons, and
it was in this time that there were giants on the earth.

'Their fall, contrary to nature's order and as a consequence, unforeseen by the supreme orderer of all things,
explains the repentance or remorse of God when it is said
that the Lord regretted having created man.

'And the text adds "On earth", for the divine plan
remained unaltered in heaven. The heavenly man had not
sinned.

'But the angel, by falling, broke the equilibrium of earth, and God was forced, so to speak, to act against his own wishes.

'For it is man's equilibrium which makes nature's balance here on earth, and if man were no longer, there would be no more world.

'For man is the receptacle of divine thought which creates and preserves the world, man is earth's *raison d'être*, all that existed before him was merely in preparation for his birth, and the entirety of creation without him would have come to nothing.

'It is thus that the prophet, in a vision, saw angels set up a throne on high, and on it was seated a figure similar to the image of a man.

'And Daniel said that he saw someone like the son of man, walking among the clouds of the sky, ascending slowly toward the Ancient of days.

'And at length he arrived before him and was made to draw nigh to the face of the Lord.'

Conclusion

'Up to this point our words have been full of mystery, hiding a higher sense, outside the grasp of most. Fortunate is he who can understand them without error!

'For these words have been given only to the masters, to the harvesters of the sacred field, to those who have undertaken the trial and come through it.

'It is written: "The ways of the Lord are straight, and the just walk in them without hindrance, but the transgressors of the law must always find there some stumbling block." '

Having said all these things, Rabbi Simeon wept and raising his voice, said: 'If some of you, oh, my brothers, are to reveal to the wicked the things you have heard, may God take you again unto himself and hide you in his glory!

'For it is better that we take leave of this world than to

reveal to the children of this world the most sublime mysteries of heaven.

'I have revealed them to you alone, in the presence of the Ancient of ancients: I have not done it for my own glory, nor for that of my father's house, nor for the honour of my brothers gathered here with me.

'But only to prevent them from straying out of the paths of great wisdom, in order that they may present themselves without shame before the gate of the holy palace, in order that they shall not be erased, like a badly formed letter, from the pages of the book of life.'

Now this is what we have learned:

Before the departure of the rabbis assembled in the enclosure, three of them died suddenly.

They were: Rabbi José

And Rabbi Thiskia

And Rabbi Jesa.

Their companions saw them lifted, carried away by holy angels beyond the veil which had been stretched over their heads.

Rabbi Simeon spoke briefly and prostrated himself.

Then he uttered a cry, saying: 'Is it true, God forgive us, that a death sentence has been pronounced against us for having revealed mysteries which have remained unknown to all men since the day when Moses, gazing face to face upon the divine image, stood before the Lord on Mount Sinai?

'If we are to be punished for this, why has not death befallen me first and why am I still among the living?'

And he heard a voice which said:

'Most fortunate are you, Rabbi Simeon, and most fortunate is your lot, as well as that of those who are with you. For there has just been revealed to you what the Lord does not reveal to all the army of heaven.

'But come and see!

'It is written: "This doctrine will fall to the eldest son, but before the youngest, the gates shall be closed."

'Those who have just died were not strong enough to carry such knowledge on the earth.

'They opened their souls to enchantment and their ecstasy carried them away.

'The holy angels took them and carried them away beyond the veil.'

Rabbi Simeon answered: 'They are happy!'

And the voice took up again: 'Go now, you who remain, for the Lord has made you strong to withstand both heaven and earth. You exist in perfect balance and harmony, and you shall live.'

They got up then, and everywhere they walked, sweet perfumes came out of the ground.

And Rabbi Simeon said: 'I see now that the earth will be blessed on our account.'

And their faces were so radiant that no one could have looked on them.

Thus it is that, as we have learned, ten entered the enclosure, but only seven came out.

Rabbi Simeon was full of joy, but Rabbi Abba felt a great sadness because of those who were no more.

But one day while the seven were seated around the master, Rabbi Simeon uttered a mysterious word.

And they saw the three who had been taken from them. Highly placed angels waited upon them, and opening golden doors, they showed them the treasures which had been laid aside for them.

Then the soul of Rabbi Abba was calmed.

From that time, the seven masters did not leave the dwelling of Rabbi Simeon.

And Rabbi Simeon said: 'We are the eyes of the Lord.'

Rabbi Abba said: 'We are six lamps who owe our light to a seventh, and this seventh is you.'

And Rabbi Jehuda called it the Great Sabbath of the week of mysteries.

One day Elijah appeared to them in his hair shirt, his face glowing with a triple light.

And Rabbi Simeon said to him: 'Were you not with us in the enclosure when we discussed the words of knowledge?'

Elijah answered: 'I wanted to be there, but the angels refused me their wings, as I had another mission to fulfill.

'On that day I went to console and deliver your brothers who are in captivity. I rubbed their chains with a balm which will one day break them.

'For the just should never be chained, unless it is with interlinking crowns.

'Thus are the days of trial linked with those of glory, and following the week of work, comes the week of rest.

'Then will every chain be as nothing before the throne of God. And when the last of the just are saved, how great will be the glory of the righteous.

'The peoples of the earth will be their crown, and they will be likened to the feast times of the Lord, sparkling from without the crown of the other days.

'A triple banquet awaits the just in the solemn rituals of the future's Great Sabbath.

'It is written: "You will call the sabbath the delight of the just and you will compare it to the holy one of God."

'Now, who is this holy one of God?

'It is Rabbi Simeon Ben-Jochai, whose name is glorified in this world and shall gather further glory in the world to come.'

Thus finishes the holy book of the Great Synod.

Part Two

Christian Glory

hristian glory is the triumph of intelligence over the beast, of truth over falsehood, of light over shadow, of humanity over the devil.
God becomes man to prevent the Devil from becoming God.

What is the Devil? It is the beast, it is shadow. It is falsehood. Why does it exist?

Because shadow is necessary as a receptacle and reflector of light, because evil is the foundation of good.

Thus are explained the shadows of the old sanctuaries, as well as the obscurities of the Bible. A shadow must exist to catch and reflect the light. The vulgar multitude has need of a terrible divinity who stirs human passions with his anger and vengeance. The exterminating God, the God of calamities is the God of shadow, the God made in the image of man, and he is the exact opposite of the God of the wise. The dark face is like a mask placed over the serene countenance of the eternal father of all beings, in order to inspire fear in disobedient children.

This doctrine should have been kept secret, for it could never be understood except by higher intellects. Unfortunately it did, in fact, creep into the world, and the result was precisely that which had been feared. Limited intellects did not understand this fictitious God with two so unlike faces, and the idea of an absurd duality sprang up in the minds of some thinkers. The dogmas of the false Zoroaster can be traced to this point. The face of light was called Ormuzd and the face of shadow became the fatal head of the dark Ahriman. Thus was the Devil created.

Note that the Bible attributes to God himself actions which might be more easily laid to the account of the usurper of the kingdom of hell. It is God who hardens Pharaoh's heart in order to punish him, together with all his people, by terrifying plagues, driving him finally to his ultimate impenitence. It is God who sends one of his messengers or angels to derange the mind of Ahab, pushing him to wage an ill-fated war. 'How will you go about it?' God asks his messenger. And the angel answers: 'I will be a spirit of untruth in the mouths of false prophets.' 'Go,' answers the Lord, 'and you will be victorious.' At this time it could not yet be imagined that the kingdom of God might be divided, nor that he kept for himself the light in order to allow his enemy to rule the realm of shadow. The God of evil had not yet been invented.

Evil, being the negation of good, can have no power; for the negation of good implies the negation of truth, whose force strikes to the very root of our being. What sort of victories might be won by a general who inevitably and voluntarily let himself be deceived? The existence of the Devil is a drastic lie. His guiding genius, if it were even possible, would be an immense madness. To struggle eternally against God, what a dream! But for this to at least appear possible, Satan must make for himself a God in his own image. He does not comprehend what even the simplest child can understand. Spirit of blindness, he is blindness personified. Curious power, to say the least: that of a blind monarch in a kingdom of shadows! All his thoughts must be false, all his efforts must be in vain: even the insane inmates of Bedlam would be justified were they to mock him.

But, one might say, there do exist here below perverse men who deny the existence of God, or, still more horrible, who believe in him and blaspheme him. The influence of these men of falsehood is great. They have a genius for destruction, they deceive, they mislead, they devour, and Providence allows them this power. Their existence and their passing triumph substantiate Satan's transitory reign. When they succeed in their calumny, in their oppression of the just, can one say, without blasphemy, that they owe their victory to God? But if it is not God who gives them the power to do evil, there must exist a dark Providence of shadows, an accursed force which God will one day vanquish, but which, for the time being, combats the very power of God and triumphs over him as soon as we give it the complicity of our hearts.

There does exist, in fact, a power which renders evil possible to a certain degree; but this power is not cursed of God, otherwise it could not exist: it is the power that God gives to any intelligent creature, that he may choose between the higher attractions of the soul and the desires born out of the base instincts of a limited nature bound to terrestrial needs. No one can love evil for evil's sake: we find at the root of all vices only ignorance and error. When one performs evil, one gives it the guise of goodness, for the very attraction inherent in disobedience is the love of freedom!

Freedom! This is the name of that power which explains evil and renders it necessary.

Freedom, which could be called man's divinity, the most beautiful, the most superb, the most irrevocable of all the Creator's gifts. Freedom which God himself cannot repress without denying his own existence. Freedom which must be won through struggle, when it is not already possessed as the supreme ruler. Freedom which is a victory, and so implies combat. The fatal attraction against which we must fight is not evil, but a blind force which must be submitted to the power coming from God that he gives to us either as a treasure or a torment, our motivating drive, which we must take hold of in order to guide it, so as not to be destroyed by it: it is a mill and we are the grain, unless we possess sufficient courage and capability to become the millers, the proprietors, those who are in control.

Theologians of the Devil, do you suppose that Satan is free? If he is, there is still time for him to revert to the paths of goodness; if he is not, he is not responsible for his actions, he is only the instrument of someone stronger than he: he is the slave of God's justice; he does nothing which God himself does not wish for. It is God who, using him, tempts, leads into sin and torments his weak creatures. Thus Satan is not the ruler of the realm of shadows, he is the agent of light behind a veil. He is of service to God, he performs God's work: God has not rejected him, for he holds him still in his hand. If God were to condemn him, he must necessarily reject him for ever. But the agent of God is the representative of God, and in accordance with all laws of logic, the representative of God is God himself.

What is the Devil, then, in the final analysis? The Devil is God working evil. A harsh and shocking definition, to be sure, for it affirms the impossible. Let us say it in a better way: the Devil is the negation of what God affirms. Now, God affirms being; thus the Devil must affirm nothingness. But nothingness can neither affirm nor be affirmed, it is nothing more than a negation, so that if the ultimate definition of God according to the Bible is this: 'He who is', the definition of the Devil must necessarily be this: 'He who is not'.

Enough, then, against this black idol, against the false god of the Persians and the Manicheans, against the colossal, nearly omnipotent Satan which superstition still dreams of. There remains to be examined Satan, chief of the Eggregores, the fallen angel who retains a shred of liberty since final judgment has not been pronounced upon him, and who profits from this delay by drawing the weak into his camp, as if he hoped to reduce the magnitude of his own sins by augmenting the number of his accomplices.

Nowhere in Genesis, nor even in the entire Bible, is allusion made to the sinfulness and fall of the angels: to find traces of this story, one must go to the apocryphal book of Enoch. This book, obviously predating the Christian era since it is cited by the apostle St Jude, held great authority in the eyes of the first Christians. Tertullian mentions it with esteem, but could not understand it, his bitter, severe genius being so foreign to the mysteries of the Qabalah, at that time preserved only by the Joannite school, albeit already deformed and profaned by the errors of Gnosticism.

The Qabalists refer all absolute ideas to the hieroglyphic and numerical value of the twenty-two letters of the primitive alphabet, which they believe to have been that of the Hebrews. A guiding genius, they say, presides over each of these letters; each letter is alive, each letter is an angel. Those who are familiar with oriental poetry should understand this figure of speech. But it is a peculiarity of the vulgar to take everything literally and to render it as tangible as possible. Now, among these letters, two represent divinity; these are the first and the last, the *aleph* and the *thau*, in Greek, the *alpha* and the *omega*, in Latin, *a* and *z*, from which has been formed the word AZOTH, in occult philosophy the expression of the absolute.

Now, the book of Enoch tells us that there existed Eggregores, that is, spirits who never sleep, heads of whole multitudes, and that twenty of these spirits dissociated themselves from their guiding principle and allowed themselves to fall.

Here is an image of the obscuring of truth in the world. Numbers detach themselves from ultimate unity. The letters of light become letters of shadow. But why?

Because the daughters of men were beautiful and the angels of heaven grew jealous of their love.

The idea was then absorbed by form, and the very principle of its beauty, exalted by beauty itself, abandoned both its guiding spirit and its ends.

The fallen angels gathered around their chief, Samiaxas, on a high mountain, which has been called ever since 'the mountain of the Oath', for the Eggregores pledged themselves there one to the other with a sacrilegious vow.

A mountain, in symbolism, represents a centre of ideas. Horeb, Sinai, Zion, Tabor, Calvary, Olympus, Parnassus, the Vatican, the Revolutionary Mountain are at the same time real and allegorical.

Some of these angels have Hebrew names, others, Persian, for in the mysterious book Abraham and Zoroaster joined forces:

The first is	Samiaxas
The second	Artakuph
The third	Arakiel
The fourth	Kababiel
The fifth	Oramammeh
The sixth	Ramiel
The seventh	Siupsick
The eighth	Zalchiel
The ninth	Balchiel
The tenth	Azazel

Now, in this inverted hierarchy, the last must necessarily occupy the position of the first. Azazel deposes Samiaxas and becomes the head of the ten primary demons. For the number ten, being the synthesis of all numbers in unity, represents the multitude, and it is well known that in the Gospels the Devel is called Legion.

The first, second, fifth and seventh Eggregores have Persian or pagan names. Why?

Because the veritable names belong to faithful angels and are unfit for fallen spirits, seeing as how *one, two, three* and *seven* are the keys to the holy numbers.

There is a second half-score of fallen spirits: these are the shadows of shadows, servants of intellectual revolt.

The first or the eleventh is called	Pharmarus
The second or the twelfth	Amariel

The third or thirteenth	Thanazael
The fourteenth	Anaguemas
The fifteenth	Samael
The sixteenth	Sarinas
The seventeenth	Ehumiel
The eighteenth	Tyriel
The nineteenth	Jamiel
The twentieth	Sariel

The meanings of these names are like those of the sacred letters, but in reverse, that is, they stand for the opposite of what is represented by pure numbers.

These spirits materialize, they take on corporeal forms in order to participate in human beauty, and the result is a race of criminals and giants, giants like the Titans of the myth, who pile up mountains to climb to heaven; in other words, spirit absorbed by matter gives disproportionate value to matter and form. This occurred in olden times and unfortunately still occurs today.

Azazel become king of the world by denying God brings dangerous knowledge and war. He teaches men to use gold, precious stones, and iron: he makes jewellery for women and weapons for men. Henceforth, men begin quarrelling over gold and women clamour for lances and swords; coquetry and duelling are inseparable. He who was to be the angel of the kingdom has become the angel of anarchy. Instead of growing more civilized, men fight, so that women may be magnificently adorned.

The eleventh angel, the one who in the Tarot corresponds to strength, taught men the art of glamour and charm, the false masks of strength. The ninth, corresponding to the number of initiation, taught them how to cause the stars to fall from the sky, that is, how to unseat the most luminous truths and drag them into the way of error. Men learned divining, using the air, the earth, the other elements, instead of simply trusting in the light of the sun. Oracles were sought in the pale reflections of the moon, and it was the seventh angel, the one of light with its seven colours, who, apostate to himself, taught this belief in the changing influences of night's beacon. Women were then initiated into the great mysteries, and men, having broken all the bonds of society and of the hierarchy, were governed by rivalry and uncontrolled greed, devouring each other. The weakest then gave forth cries of anguish towards heaven, and the four angels of harmony – those which represent the letters of the divine Tetragrammation: Michael, the angel of the letter *yod*, the father-spirit, creativity as an active force; Gabriel, the angel of the letter *he*, representing the mother, creativity as a passive force; Raphael, the angel of the letter *van*, the spirit of creative work; and Uriel, the angel of generating fire – touched by the plaintive cries of man, came to the foot of the throne of God and begged him to put a stop to the frightful disorderliness of the world. It was then that God announced his plan to purify the earth by means of the flood, in order to suppress the cursed race of the giants. And seeking to save the oppressed, he saw that they also were cowardly and wicked, and he found only the family of Noah to be worthy of mercy before the Lord.

And God said to Raphael, the angel of true knowledge and of pure initiation, he who governs the planet Mercury, the sacred spirit of the triple Hermes: 'Go, lay hold of Azazel and cast him, bound hand and foot, into the darkness. You will also bind closed his eyes, so that henceforth he shall see no more light; then, striking the earth with your foot, you will make a great abyss in the desert of Dodoel. There you will hurl him down upon the sharp rocks and pointed stones, and this will be the end of him for ever.

'Then, on the day of the great judgment, he will be called to answer for his crimes, and so condemned to eternal fire.

'As for you, make known on the earth the ways of health, give the world medicine for its wounds. And bring back to the side of truth the revelations of Azazel, which have brought about so many sins among men.'

Further on, the author of the book of Enoch adds this remarkable passage:

'The souls of the giants, born of an unholy alliance, are half spiritual and half material; their impure origin makes them evil, and these are the wicked spirits who wander through the atmosphere. Natural enemies of justice, they originate perverse forces and powerful currents of evil. They subsist without food and will not touch sacrificial flesh. They cause visions and give rise to phantoms whose property it is to change shape, but with a tendency to dwindle and fade. They are dead, moreover, and are to be one day resurrected with the other children of men.'

Here is certainly a terrifying revelation for raisers of spirits and amateur spiritualists. What we have called in our earlier works ghosts and vampires, coagulations and unhealthy projections of astral light, are in reality, according to the book of Enoch, monstrous hybrid souls formed out of the commerce of the Eggregores with prostitutes of the ancient world; the souls of giants exterminated in the flood, unwholesome exhalations of the earth and of the venom of the serpent, Python.

Three remarks must be made on this obviously ancient legend:

1. The facts thus recounted are allegorical, as in the Apocalypse and the tales of the Talmud. These are metamorphoses after the fashion of Ovid: it is impossible for beings, whoever and whatever they are, to change their nature. It would be utterly in vain for a man to fall in love with a graceful dove, he could never become one himself, and even if he could, it does not follow that the dove could give birth to other types of birds. The same must be said for these so-called angels, immaterial spirits who mythically fell in love with women and so transformed themselves into men, thus spawning the race of giants.

2. It must not be supposed that angels ever wished to dethrone God, revolting against him: this is a monstrous

and impossible idea, borrowed from the Titans of Greek mythology. The Titans can, according to legend, climb to the heights of Olympus, but can one imagine a host of angels declaring war on infinity?

3. Finally, the spirit of false knowledge (become man, let us not forget), was thrown before the flood, bound hand and foot, into the abyss where he must remain until the day of judgment. Therefore, he has nothing in common with Satan who wanders about the earth tempting mankind, and the book of Enoch, even were it to be taken literally rather than apocryphally, proves nothing in favour of the modern Devil.

Satan is mentioned in the book of Job, but there he does not play the role of an angel cast out of the heavens and banned for ever from the presence of God. He is, rather, a kind of public prosecutor who dwells among the Beni-Elohim, that is, the sons of God. The Lord speaks to him, asks him questions and gives him missions to carry out. He wanders through the earth and returns before Adonai to give account of what he has seen. He is ordered to test Job, and the power behind all these trials, Satan, brings down upon the head of this holy man all the evil possible. Job is victorious over all and God rewards him; but Satan has gained neither punishment nor blame, he has only obeyed God.

The book of Job is, moreover, simply an allegory whose meaning is to show that evil on earth is a test of virtue. All the characters in this oriental poem are symbolic, even their names make this clear. Job, is the afflicted; Satan stands, in general, for the test, and in particular, for calumny. The details of the story are as ridiculous as those of a fable, but the philosophical meaning is quite beautiful. Out of all this, in any case, nothing reasonable can be concluded as to the real existence of a being named Satan.

In Moses's book of Genesis, it is the serpent who tempts woman. Now, this serpent, in the sacred myths of antiquity, sometimes represents fire, sometimes the vital fluid, the flowing force of terrestrial life. In Greek mythology, Vulcan, god of fire, angers Jupiter because of his ugliness, and the master of Olympus hurls him down with a single blow. He is the husband of Venus who tempts mortals and leads them astray, he lives in caverns full of flames where he busies himself by forging weapons and thunderbolts, thereby laying the way for war and violent storms.

In the Gospels, Jesus gives out this profound oracle of eternal wisdom:

'The Devil is a liar, together with his father.'

The Devil, whatever he may be, cannot then be one of God's creatures, at least in his quality as the Devil.

But what is this father of the Devil? The father of the Devil is falsehood.

He is, himself, falsehood and the father of falsehood.

Compared to He who is, he deserves to be called he who is not; and yet he has an actual existence.

Let us explain this seeming contradiction. He does not exist, cannot exist as a single and powerful personality.

Hell is anarchy, and there is no other king of hell than the image of the dark God such as Rabbi Simeon explains it.

Satan is not the Ahriman of the Persians, nor the Anti-god of the Manicheans; he was never an angel of light, for his light is only an hallucination of the wicked.

He was never a creative spirit, for he is nothing more than an immense folly.

But he is a force, a terrible one, calculating, crafty, taking on a thousand forms and entering freely everywhere, sometimes threatening, sometimes cajoling, always powerful; a force desired by God when he gave liberty to man, although it is a force which inevitably produces bondage; a force which takes on a personification among the vast multitudes who voluntarily go astray. In the Gospels, the Saviour asks him his name and he answers: 'I am called Legion, for I am many.'

The Devil is the beast, or rather, the beastliness, the stupidity which governs the multitudes: he is *the attraction, the fatal magnetism of evil.*

This magnetism of evil makes it possible for all subjects of the dark kingdom, or better, of shadowy anarchy, to understand each other from one end of the world to the other without speaking. It leads astray the pagans, these persecutors of the Christians, as well as the Christians themselves, persecutors of free-thought. It has come into the world under the names of Nero, of Torquemada, of Proud'hon and of Veuillot. It has furnished soldiers to the Pope and false prophets to the partisans of independant morality. It is positivist with Littré, spiritist with Allan-Kardec, diabolist with de Mirville and Gougenot-Desmousseaux. It regrets nothing so much as the axes of the Committee for Public Health, unless it is the pyres of St Dominic and of Pius V. Under two different guises, it has presided over the congress of Malines and the congress of Geneva, for its transformations are prompt and elusive. It inspires the foolish and attempts to paralyse the wise. Its character is always that of evil or stupidity. It loves despotism and anarchy equally; what it hates above all is reason. It is willing that Desbarreaux be an atheist, provided that Pascal be Jansenist. With Ravaillac and Damiens it takes the form of bigotry, with Robespierre and Marat, philosophy. It is the serpent of a thousand colours and coils, he guides his forked tongue and flattened head everywhere. He drools venom on all that is pure, tears down all that is beautiful, draws to himself all shame and ugliness. He follows men everywhere, he can be encountered at all times: one might say that the entire world is his. He is more horrible than horror, more fearsome than fear, deadlier than death. He is the father of nightmares, the king of treacherous visions: he is a dwarf and a giant. Now he is a Typhoeus with a thousand heads, now he is an all but invisible scorpion who scurries beneath your feet. Callot and Goya only half glimpsed his grotesque transformations. Dante in his dream saw only a portion of his dreadfulness, and the sculptors of our cathedral portals have never succeeded in carving his utter ugliness. For who can sound the bottom of all folly? To whom has fever breathed its final word? Give a body of pain and torture to nothingness and tell me just how far towards impossibility hideous distortion can go. Then I will answer: 'There is the Devil, there is the pontiff of black magic; there is the one sorcerers call up, the one who appears to them, promising treasure, only to cast them into the abyss!'

The magnetic force, this powerful vehicle of thought and life, has been placed by nature in the service of man's will: our virtues and our perversities together determine its currents. The sacred serpent of Aesculapius has the same symbolic form as the serpents of Tisiphone, Moses himself, who tells us how a serpent introduced sin and death into the world, had erected the image of a bronze serpent to cure those victims mortally wounded by snake-bite in the desert.

The catholic, that is, universal dogma has not yet been formulated in the Church except as a mystery. It is accepted without being understood, even by faith, for it has been imposed without the acceptance of the free concourse of reason. It seems, in fact, sometimes to contradict knowledge, for we have not yet learned to distinguish history from allegory, or mystic fictions, however perceptive, from scientific realities which remain inaccessible to the onslaught of faith. If someone tells me, for example, that a Virgin has become a mother while remaining a virgin, that a child has come out of her as a ray of sunlight passes through a crystal without breaking it, I respect and admire this image: but I cannot, unless I were a fool, believe that it is a question of a material and natural childbirth, for I know that such circumstances cannot be. When the Bible tells me that the mountains leapt like rams and the hills like lambs, I do not take this literally. When I find that Joshua stopped the sun in its course (and alas! it is for this that Galilee has been condemned!), I understand that we are dealing with an expression characteristic of oriental poetry and which signifies that the exploits of the Hebrews on that day doubled or tripled the 'value' of the day. Napoleon I was perhaps also not far from believing he commanded the sun on the day of the battle of Austerlitz.

If we read in the symbolic statement of Nicaea that the son of God was born of the father before the beginning of all time and if we are simultaneously taught that he is eternal like the father, we must understand that this birth has nothing whatsoever to do with a normal, material one, since it is a question of a birth that is not even a beginning. If we find later in this same statement that this selfsame son of God came down from heaven for ourselves and for the salvation of mankind, are we to imagine infinity coming down from above? Relative to God, is heaven up above and the earth below? Expressions of faith, then, have no connection with those of knowledge or science, and the same words, used in explaining dogma, do not necessarily always mean the same thing.

The Church, to use the words of the prophet David, officially calls the Devil the arrow which flies by day and the nameless thing which wanders by night. Elsewhere he is called, still more remarkably, the impetuous current and the spirit of great heat (*ab incursu* and *daemonio meridiano*). St Paul says we must combat the powers of our atmosphere (*potestates aeris hujus*).

Is it not clear that these designations refer to forces rather than to persons? And so what does it matter that in its exorcisms the Church should speak to the demon as to a person capable of hearing? Are the sea and the winds also persons? Yet we see that in the Gospels Jesus Christ speaks to them, saying, 'Wind, be still; sea, be calm,' and in addition, that the sea and the wind, as if capable of hearing, quieted immediately.

The Gospels, which St Jean calls the eternal Gospels, are

not the story of a man named Jesus, but the symbolic
history of the son of God, the legend of the eternal Word.
The stars of the sky wrote this all before the birth of man
and the magi had already seen it there when they came to
adore the living materialization. Egypt's hieroglyphics are
full of it. Isis nursing Horus is as gentle as the Virgin
mother, crowned with stars and with the moon beneath
her feet. Devaki presenting her chaste breast to Krishna is
worshipped by wise men of India, who have also preserved
the story in their gospels. The stories of Krishna and Christ
seem copied one from the other. The Indian fable even
contains Moses's serpent and the struggles of the Saviour
against Satan. The Gospels are the eternal Genesis of
liberty; the tender triumph of spirit over brute matter.

This is a description and a condemnation of the
ephemeral reign of Satan, that is, of falsehood and of
tyranny. In our book entitled *The Science of Spirit* we
discussed this truth, comparing the texts of the canonical
Gospels and the apocryphal Gospels. We are going to
complete our work here by giving the most remarkable
passages of this marvellous Indian fable which we might be
tempted to call the Gospel of Krishna.

The Legend of Krishna
Selection from the Bhagavadam

CHAPTER I
The Conception

The soul of the earth complained to Brahma, saying: 'The
race of giants, the children of iniquity have grown
infinitely numerous.

'Their pride is unbearable and I wail, oppressed by the
weight of their iniquity. Come to my aid, oh, Brahma!'

Then Brahma, accompanied by all the gods, betook
himself to that mysterious sea whose waves are of milk and

upon which Vishnu reposes in glory and beatitude.

Standing near this glitteringly white sea, Brahma meditated upon himself, worshipping himself in the divine Trimurti; then, revealing the mysteries of supreme will, he said: 'Vishnu shall become man.'

Then the serpent, Scissia, made its hiss heard and Brahma said to it: 'You will become man at the same time, in order to perpetuate his glory, and he will triumph over you and over fatality, your sister.

'He will be called Krishna, which is to say, Azure, for he will be the son of the heavens.

'Wisemen and patriarchs, return upon the earth to worship him; make shepherds of yourselves, for such will he be.'

Oh! who can speak worthily of the acts of this God? Those who fill themselves with this divine story will be submerged in an ocean of delights. The evils of this world and those to come will no longer have a hold on them. This man-God advances, his large eyes full of majesty; a smile is on his lips, a mark stands in the centre of his forehead and his curly hair drifts gracefully down. Those who have looked upon him cannot ever wish to turn away their eyes. May his image be engraved on every heart! May the memory of this God, of this infant shepherd, brought up by cattle and lambs, be ever present to all spirits of heaven and earth!

CHAPTER II
The Nativity

Cangassem, king of Madura, having learned that the beautiful Devaki, wife of Vassondeva, was to bring a child into the world who would one day replace him, resolved to kill the infant as soon as it was born.

However when the time came, Vishnu filled Vassondeva with his light, and Vassondeva concentrated and reflected this light into the chaste breast of Devaki.

Devaki thus became with child in a wholly celestial fashion and without the ordinary workings of man.

Cangassem then ordered that she be put in prison; but when the hour of the birth of Krishna was come, the prison opened of itself, and the infant-God was transported to the stable of Nanden where he lay surrounded by shepherds.

Brahma, Shiva and the other gods came to worship him in this humble shelter, showering him with flowers. The angels, Gheadaruver, sang, danced and played the most melodious of instruments. All stars and planets were at this time aligned in favourable aspect. Vassondeva prostrated himself before this divine child, worshipped him and said: 'Oh, you who have engendered Brahma and who are born here among us, here you lie imprisoned in a mortal body, governed by destiny and open to the accidents befalling matter, you who are not material, inaccessible to death; the hour draws nigh when Cangassem will come to kill you. Make it possible for us to save your life and ours with you!'

Devaki made a similar prayer; then Krishna opened his mouth and spoke. He reassured his parents, revealed to them the supreme destinies, and having promised them eternal blessedness, he retreated again into silence, behaving normally as any child.

CHAPTER III
The Massacre of the Innocents

Now Cangassem, having learned that Devaki had given birth, ran to the prison and thought he saw her lying there with a child beside her. A mule nearby began to bray, and the tyrant believed this to be a warning from heaven. He drew his sword. It was in vain that Devaki showed him the child was only a girl; Cangassem threw her into the air and held out his sword in order to catch her again on its point. But the infant, soaring above his head, cried, 'I am Fatality. Tremble and quake, for your future conqueror is hidden in an inaccessible retreat, and henceforth until the hour of your punishment, I shall remain suspended over you.'

Cangassem was afraid and prostrated himself at Devaki's feet. He offered her gifts as well as her freedom to escape with Vassondeva where she might choose. However Krishna grew and remained hidden.

Cangassem was tortured by fear; he grew furious and commanded, throughout all his states, the massacre of every newborn child.

Only the young Krishna escaped the king's assassins. The giants of evil, for their part, also plotted his loss. One day one of them came in the form of a terrible chariot, rolling violently forward towards the infant as if to crush him. Krishna held out his foot, smiling, and as soon as this tiny foot touched the chariot, it broke into a thousand pieces which fell around the divine child without touching him.

Another giant, running with the speed of the wind, carried off Krishna, setting him on his shoulders and taking him to the middle of the sea to drown him. But the child grew so heavy that the giant, bent beneath the weight, was drowned himself, and Krishna returned to dry land, walking on the water.

CHAPTER IV
Childhood Anecdotes Similar
to Those of the Gospels

Krishna, wishing in his childhood to appear as other children of men, often played mischievous tricks which astonished his parents themselves, but which always ended advantageously. One day, for example, he made off with the clothes of several girls who were swimming, and to have them back, they were obliged to stand immobile, their eyes raised towards heaven and their hands joined above their heads. Thus they were made to blush over their immodesty, but also were taught the attitude of prayer.

He took milk and butter from the rich, giving them to the less fortunate. One day, to punish him for this, he had been chained to a millstone; he broke his chain, picked up the stone and threw it against two large trees which were felled by the blow. But out of these two trees came two men who worshipped the child and said to him: 'Be praised! You are our saviour! We are Nalacon ben and Manicrida, and as punishment for our faults, we were imprisoned in these trees. For us to regain our freedom, a God had to come and cast them down.'

Another time, the trees and fields caught fire; the young Krishna, smiling, parted his lips and gently breathed in the flame. The entire holocaust detached itself then from the earth and came to die on the scarlet lips of Krishna.

Brahma, as a trial, had hidden the flocks which had been entrusted to his guard. Krishna made lambs of clay and gave them life. Brahma declared himself conquered and gave back the flocks he had hidden, proclaiming Krishna the creator and master of all things.

Not long after, the animals and shepherds, having drunk from the river of Colinady, died instantly; for Nakuendra, king of serpents, vanquished by Gheronda, prince of the Misans, had hid himself in the waters of this river. Krishna came down to the banks. Immediately the king of serpents threw himself upon him and surrounded him with his coils. But Krishna disengaged himself, forced the reptile to bend down his head, climbed upon it and, holding himself thus upright in the middle of the waters, began to play the flute. Immediately the shepherds and flocks who had died were brought back to life. Vishnu pardoned the serpent, who, having lost his venom, could do no more harm; but he ordered him to withdraw to the isle of Ratnagaram.

CHAPTER V
The Baptism

Devendra, god of the waters, feeling himself neglected because of Krishna, the honours due him unpaid, caused it to rain for seven days and seven nights in order to submerge the shepherds' fields: but Krishna, lifting with one hand the mountain of Gavertonam, set it between the sky and the earth. Devendra then recognized his powerlessness and, prostrating himself before Krishna, he said to him: 'Oh, Krishna, you are the supreme Being; you have neither desire nor passion; however, you act as if you did. You protect the righteous and punish the wicked. Only one of your moments contains Brahma in infinite repetition. Save me, oh, you, whose eyes have the sweetness of the tamarisk's flower!'

Krishna smiled and answered: 'Oh, prince among the gods, I humiliated you to make you greater. For I bring low him whom I wish to save: be gentle and humble of heart.'

Devendra spoke again: 'I am commanded by Brahma to consecrate you and recognize you as the king of Brahmins, as the good shepherd of all sheep and as the master of all souls who seek mildness and peace.'

Then he arose, gave him holy unction and named him shepherd of shepherds.

CHAPTER VI
The Song of Songs

Krishna was playing the pastoral flute and all the young women were following him. Young girls, in order to hear him, left the homes of their fathers.

And Krishna said to them:

'Oh, women, do you not fear the anger of your husbands? Young maidens, do you not dread the reproach of your fathers? Return to those who have reason to be jealous of your love.'

And the women said, and the young girls answered:

'If we left our husbands and fathers for a man, we would be wicked: but how can mortals have the right to be jealous of the love which draws us to a god?'

Then Krishna, seeing to what degree their desires were pure, gave them all his tenderness. He satisfied them all in his divine embrace, and all of them were happy; but each of them believed herself alone to be the faithful companion and chaste spouse of Krishna.

CHAPTER VII
The Transfiguration

A great sacrificial feast was to take place at Madura and the king Cangassem invited Krishna in order to have an opportunity to kill him.

The giant Acrura came before him with his cart on which Krishna did not refuse to mount.

The river Emuneh was on the way, and Acrura, having got down to bathe himself, saw Krishna mirrored in the waves, glowing with pure light. On his forehead, the God had a triple diadem. His four arms were thickly covered with bracelets of pearls. Sparkling eyes glittered like precious stones over his whole body, and his hands stretched in all directions to the very limits of the universe. The heart of Acrura was then changed, and when he found Krishna seated calmly on his cart, he worshipped him sincerely and wished for him that he escape the traps laid by the old Cangassem and that he exit victorious from this most dangerous of trials.

CHAPTER VIII
The Triumphal Entry

Then Krishna made his entry into the royal city of Madura. He was poorly clothed, as are all shepherds ordinarily, and the first thing he encountered were slaves bearing on a wagon the clothes of the king. 'The king's clothes are mine,' said Krishna; but the slaves only laughed at him.

Then he stretched out his hand and they fell dead, the wagon toppled over and the royal vestments came by themselves to lie at the feet of Krishna.

Seeing this, all the inhabitants of the city came to offer him gifts. Vases of gold and silver, most precious jewels awaited him along the path he was to take; but he did not deign to stoop and take them. A poor gardener named Sandama came in his turn and offered Krishna his most beautiful flowers. The God stopped then, gathered up this poor man's offering and asked him what he might desire in exchange. 'I ask that your name be glorified,' said Sandama. 'I ask that the entire world love you; and as for myself, I entreat you to make me more and more open to the cries of the unfortunate.' Krishna saw then that he loved Sandama and came to rest several hours in his house.

CHAPTER IX
Krishna Triumphs Over All the Giants

Cangassem perished while seeking to kill Krishna, and the young God freed Cangassem's father from prison and restored his kingdom which his son had usurped; then he returned to solitude and gave himself over to the study of the Vedas. Giants made war on him and were all conquered. One day they had surrounded the mountain where he had retired with fire and they laid siege to it with innumerable armies. Krishna rose above the flames, and having made himself invisible, passed through the very midst of the enemy and withdrew to another solitary place.

However it was written in the heavens that Krishna was to die in order to atone for the sins of his race. His parents were of the tribe of the Yadavers, which was to grow so numerous as to cover the whole of the earth. But proud of their numbers and their riches, they insulted the prophets of Ixora, and the terrible God caused a great iron sceptre to fall among them, saying: 'Here is the rod which shall break the pride and hope of the Yadavers.'

They consulted Krishna, and he advised them to dissolve the iron rod, reducing it to dust. They did this and the iron powder was thrown into the water; but as it happened, one sharp splinter had been overlooked in the dissolving of the sceptre. A fish, having swallowed it, was wounded and taken by a fisherman who withdrew the iron needle and affixed it to the end of an arrow. And all this was accomplished by the will of the gods who, for the salvation of the world and the deliverance of Vishnu, were laying plans for the death of Krishna.

CHAPTER X
Words Before the Passion

It is also told that an ugly and misformed woman carrying a vase of sweet-smelling oil of great price came to Krishna and poured it out upon his head. Immediately her ugliness disappeared, her deformities vanished, and she went away endowed with wonderful beauty.

However, the hour of the great sacrifice was approaching: signs and wonders appeared in heaven and on earth. Owls cried in the full light of day and ravens croaked the night through; horses spit fire, raw harvested rice sprouted, the globe of the sun was tinged with many colours.

Krishna threatened the Yadavers with impending destruction and counselled them to leave their city in order to escape the plagues which were to befall it; but they did not listen, and having grown divise among themselves, they took up weapons, hard pointed sticks like swords which might have been born from the iron rod that had been ground to dust and cast upon the water. The sceptre of despotism had been destroyed, but from its dust had arisen civil war and anarchy.

Krishna had a favourite disciple named Ontaven. This disciple asked him for some instruction, that he might keep it in his memory, and Krishna said to him: 'In seven days the city of Danvaragay will be destroyed. The Calyugam will begin its course. In this new age, men will be wicked, without truth and without mutual goodwill. They will be physically weak, full of illness and of short life; thus, leave the world entirely behind and retire to a solitary place; there you will think always of me, you will forsake the pleasures of the world and reform your souls through attentive meditation. Learn to live in thought; believe that the universe is in me, that it has no existence except through me; triumph over maya which is only the illusion of appearances; keep company with wise men, that I may be always in you and you in me. He who renounces the vanity of falsehood for the truth which gives wisdom will draw unto himself the divine light. His heart will become as pure as a perfectly calm sea, and he will be a reflection of my image.

'Renounce entirely the spirit of possession of temporal things; this is the first step in the way of perfection; it is by absolute detachment that the passions can be mastered.

'The soul is the sovereign of the senses, and I am the sovereign of the soul.

'Space is greater than the elements, and I am greater than space.

'Will is stronger than all obstacles, and I am the master of will.

'Brahma is greater than the gods, and I am greater than Brahma.

'The sun is the most luminous of all the other stars, and I am more luminous and life-giving than the sun.

'In words, I am truth; in vows, I am he who orders that nothing having life be killed; in charity, I am the gift of bread; among the seasons, I am the springtime which gives life. Truth, wisdom, love, charity, goodness, prayer, the Vedas, Eternity, these are my images.'

Having received these instructions, Ontaven withdrew into the desert of Badary.

CHAPTER XI
The Death of Krishna

Krishna then returned to the Yadavers, those of his own race, and found they had exterminated each other entirely. The country they had lived in was no longer anything more than a field covered with bodies of the dead. He raised his eyes and saw the souls of those he had loved on earth returning to heaven.

Finding himself alone and sad, he lay down at the foot of a mysterious bush whose powerful roots ran visibly along the ground and whose branches, covered with red leaves and thorns, twisted far away in all directions. Krishna lay full length near the trunk of the bush, his feet crossed and of his four hands, two extended in an attitude of worship, two joined in prayer. An arrow came then by chance and struck him; an aimless arrow shot by a hunter came to fasten the crossed feet of Krishna to the bush. It was the arrow which had been made with the sharp fragment of the sceptre that Krishna had broken. This was the final vengeance of tyranny and death.

Hardly had he died than the thrones of the unjust toppled of themselves, his body disappeared suddenly and was miraculously found in Geganadam where a temple was built to him and where he has since been worshipped under the name of Jagganath.

This legend is taken from the Baghavadam, one of the Puranas, the holy books of the Indians, to which they attribute the very greatest antiquity. We have divided it into chapters to which we have given titles indicative of the connections that may be made with our Gospels, whose spirit is clearly manifest in this wonderful ideal of divine incarnation. What foolish brahmin could ever take this sacred poetry for history? None-the-less, will not India someday produce its own Renan who will write, choosing this and ignoring that, a colourless and prosaic life of Krishna?

Part Three

The Flaming Star

he flaming star is a Masonic symbol which represents the absolute in being, in truth, in reality, in reason and in justice. (*See the figure at the beginning of our history of magic.*)

Among the mysteries of Masonic initiation, there is a mysterious and obviously quite ancient legend which sheds light on the high philosophy of the Gospels and which tells of the eternal martyrdom of righteousness for ever oppressed by evil, but for ever triumphant over it. In this legend, it is envy, cupidity and pride which are the three heads of the infernal demon, but this demon is the spirit-genius of perverse men, represented by the three traitors. We are speaking here of the legend of Hiram.

Masonic philosophy, the same as that of the ancient Qabalah, is a protestation against cults which constitute an outrage to nature. Its basis is eternal order. Its guiding principle is the immutable justice which presides over the laws of the universe; it rejects all idea of caprice and privilege; it teaches equality within the hierarchic order, it regards as a necessity the degrees of initiation and the classification of brothers by order of knowledge and merit; it admits, finally, all beliefs, but it rectifies them through faith in the eternal order.

Among its symbols, it admits the cross, sign of sacrifice

and death, but united with the rose, which represents love and life. The square and the compass, these represent justliness united with justness. Masonic philosophy points out the dogmas which divide priests and pastors into factions, these men who exist ostensibly to bring unity to mankind. It preaches to all charity and goodwill.

Freemasonry is the first attempt at universal synthesis and truly catholic association. We are aware that this name seems to belie the thing; but this illogicity. must be taken into consideration: the so-called Catholics are the most exclusive of men and the Freemasons who, under the guise of the profane, seem to exist at the fringes of human majority, are in reality the only serious partisans of universal alliance.

To reconcile Freemasonry and Catholicism what would be necessary? Bringing mutual distrust to a halt and the cultivation of mutual understanding. For these two contrary but not contradictory doctrines are at bottom the double solution of a single problem: the reconciliation of reason and faith. But how to reconcile opposites? We have already said it: never to confuse them, but always to associate them, remembering this great axiom of occult philosophy — harmony results from the analogy of opposites.

Masonic Legends

Extracts from a Ritual
Manuscript of the Eighth Century

First Legend

Solomon, the wisest of all the kings of his time, wanting to build a temple to the Eternal, assembled together in Jerusalem all suitable workers for the construction of this edifice. He had an edict published throughout his kingdom and which spread thence over the entire world: that whoever wished to come to Jerusalem to work on the building of the temple would be well received and recompensed, on the condition that he be virtuous, full of zeal and courage and not subject to any vice. Soon Jerusalem was filled with a multitude of men who were aware of the noble virtues of Solomon and who asked to be inscribed as workers on the temple. Solomon, having thus assured himself of a large number of workmen, made treaties with all the neighbouring kings, in particular with the king of Tyre, to the effect that he might select from Mount Lebanon all the cedars and other woods and materials necessary.

The work was already under way when Solomon remembered a man named Hiram, in architecture the most knowledgeable man of his time, and wise and virtuous as well, one who, because of his fine qualities, had found favour with the king of Tyre. He noted also that so great a number of workers could not carry on their work without a great deal of difficulty and confusion; thus the temple's progress was beginning to be greatly hampered by the discussions which took place among them. Solomon resolved, then, to give them a chief capable of maintaining order, and chose this man Hiram, an Ethirian by nationality. He sent deputies loaded with gifts to the king of Tyre, asking him to send the famous architect called Hiram. The king of Tyre, delighted with the esteem Solomon showed him, accorded his request, sending him back Hiram and his deputies burdened with riches and instructed to tell the ruler that beyond the treaty they had made together, he accorded Solomon an alliance for ever, placing at his disposition all that might be found in his kingdom which could prove useful. The deputies arrived in Jerusalem, along with Hiram, on 15 July . . . , a beautiful summer day. They entered Solomon's palace. Hiram was received with all the pomp and magnificence due his great virtues. The same day Solomon gave a feast for all the temple workers in honour of his arrival.

The next day Solomon called together the Chamber of Advisers to settle matters of importance; Hiram was among them and received with favour. Solomon said to him before all present: 'Hiram, I chose you as chief and head architect for the temple, as I chose each of the workers. I give you full power over them, your decisions will be final; thus I regard you as my friend to whom I would confide the greatest of my secrets.' Next they left the council chamber and went to the temple's site where Solomon himself said in a loud and intelligible voice to all the workers, showing Hiram to them: 'Here is the man I have chosen as your chief, it is he who shall guide you; you will obey him as you would me. I give him full power over you and over the work. All dissention as regards my orders or his shall be punished in whatever manner he sees fit.' Then they made a tour of the work that had been done; and all was put into Hiram's hands, and Hiram promised the king that all would soon return to order.

The following day Hiram called together all the workers and said to them: 'My friends, the King, our master, has put me in charge of maintaining order among you and of regulating all work on the temple. I have no doubt that all of you are filled with zeal to execute his orders and mine. There are those among you who deserve distinguished salaries; each of you may achieve this, the proof will be in your work. It is for your own peace of mind and to honour your zeal that I am going to form three classes out of all of you: the first will be composed of apprentices, the second, of fellows, and the third, of masters.

'The first will be paid accordingly and will receive its salary at the gate of the temple, column J.

'Likewise the second at the gate of the temple, column B.

'And the third in the sanctuary of the temple.'

Payment was higher in accordance with rank, and each of the workers was happy to accept the authority of so worthy a chief. Peace, friendship and concord reigned among them. The good Hiram, wanting that all remain orderly and wishing to prevent any confusion among the workers, applied to each rank signs, words and gestures by which its members could recognize each other. They were prohibited, however, from confiding these to any others without express permission of the king or of their chief. Thus they received their salary only upon giving their sign; and the masters were paid as masters, the fellows as fellows, and the apprentices as apprentices. In accordance with so perfect a system, each continued in peace, and the work progressed steadily as Solomon desired it should.

But could so fine an order remain for long without upset and revolution? No. Three fellows, impelled by avarice and envy to receive the pay of masters, resolved to learn the necessary word; and as they could only obtain it from the respectable master Hiram, it became their design to get it from him either willingly or by force. Since the good Hiram went daily into the sanctuary of the temple towards five o'clock in the evening in order to make his prayers to the Eternal, they agreed together to wait for his exit, and then to ask him the word of the masters. There being three doors to the temple, one to the east, one to the west and the other to the south, they stationed themselves individually, one at each of the doors, armed respectively with a measuring stick, an iron rod and a mallet; and they waited.

Hiram, having finished his prayer, made to exit by the southern door where he encountered one of the traitors, armed with a measuring stick, who stopped him and demanded to know the master's word. Hiram, astonished, was quick to point out that it was not in this way that he might obtain the secret, that he would, in fact, sooner die than give it out. The traitor, maddened by this refusal, struck him with his stick. Hiram, stunned by the blow, withdrew into the temple and made for the western door where he met with the second traitor who demanded the

same as the first. Hiram remained firm in his refusal,
angering this second man who struck him a blow with his
metal bar. Hiram stumbled back inside and, certain of
success this time, made his way to the eastern door. But
here he encountered the third traitor who repeated the
same demand. Hiram told him that he preferred death to
revealing to him a secret he did not yet merit, and this
traitor, outraged by such a refusal, gave him so great a
blow with his mallet that he killed him. As it was still day,
the traitors took the body of Hiram and hid it in a pile of
waste north of the temple, waiting for the fall of night in
order to transport it further away. And accordingly, when
it was dark, they carried it out of the city on to a high
mountain where they buried it. Deciding that they would
take it even further away one day, they planted on the
grave an acacia branch so as to be able to recognize the
place, and then they returned to Jerusalem.

The good Hiram was in the habit of going daily, first
thing in the morning, to Solomon, giving him an account
of the work, and receiving his orders. Not seeing Hiram on
the following day, Solomon sent one of his officers to
fetch him, but the man returned saying he had searched
everywhere and that no one had been able to find him.
This answer saddened Solomon, who went himself to look
for him in the temple and had a thorough search made of
all the city. The third day, Solomon, having gone to pray
in the temple's sanctuary, came out by the eastern door.
There he was surprised to see a few traces of blood. He
followed them to the pile of waste on the building's
northern side, and had it searched, nothing was found,
except that the rubbish itself had been recently disturbed.
He trembled with horror and concluded that Hiram had
been murdered. He went back into the sanctuary to mourn
the loss of so great a man, then out into the court of the
temple where he called together all the masters, saying to
them: 'My brothers, the loss of your chief is a certainty.'
At these words, each of them fell into a deep sadness,

which brought about a long period of silence, interrupted at last by Solomon, saying that nine from among them must leave in search of Hiram's body, which once found should be brought back inside the temple.

Solomon had scarcely finished speaking when all the masters voiced their desire to go, even the oldest, without regard for difficulty of the surrounding roads. Seeing their zeal, Solomon repeated that only nine of them would leave and these would be chosen by vote. Those whom chance selected for the search were so transported by joy that they undid their sandals so as to be more agile and set out directly. Three took the road to the south, three the road to the west, and three that to the east, promising one another to meet in the north on the ninth day of their walk. Eventually one of them sat down to rest, and finding himself quite tired and wishing to stretch out on the ground, took hold of an acacia branch for support; but the branch, freshly planted, remained in his hand. This, of course, surprised him, and it was then that he saw a rather large space of newly turned earth and deduced that Hiram was buried in this place.

His strength renewed and animated by courage, he rejoined the other masters who came together, explained what had happened, and they all began to dig in the ground, enlivened with a single purpose. The body of the good Hiram was, in fact, buried in this spot, and when they uncovered it at last, they recoiled in horror, trembling. Then sorrow took hold of their hearts and they wept a long time; but at last they found again their courage. One of them went into the grave and took hold of Hiram by the right index finger, thinking to raise him. But Hiram's flesh was already in a state of decomposition and foul smelling, which made him fall back, saying 'Iclinque', which means 'he smells'. Another took hold of him by the finger next to the index; but the same thing happened to him as had happened to the first, and he withdrew, saying 'Jakin'. (The response is: Boaz.)

The masters held a consultation. Since they did not know that in dying, Hiram had preserved the secrecy of the master's word, they resolved to change it, deciding that the first word uttered when the body was raised from its tomb would be the new word from then on. Then the oldest one of them entered the grave and gripped the good Hiram just above the right wrist, pressing their chests together, his left hand behind the cadaver's back and against its shoulder, and in this way he lifted Hiram from the ground. His body made a muffled sound which frightened them, but the master, still full of courage, cried 'Mac-Benack', which means, 'the flesh comes away from the bones'. Next they repeated the word one to another, embracing one another, then took up the body of the good Hiram and transported it back to Jerusalem. They arrived in the middle of the night, but the moon was exceedingly bright, and they entered the temple where they set the body down. Informed of their arrival, Solomon came to the temple, accompanied by all the masters, all attired in an apron and white gloves, where they gave the last honours to the good Hiram. Solomon had him buried in the sanctuary and had placed on his tomb a gold plate, triangular in shape, wherein was engraved in Hebrew the name of the Eternal. Then he rewarded the masters with compasses of gold which they attached to their garments by means of a blue ribbon; and they exchanged the new words, signs and gestures.

These same ceremonies are performed when, on the occasion of his reception, the candidate is lifted from a coffin.

The password is Gibline, the name of the village nearest to where Hiram's body was found.

Second Legend

Having laid Hiram's body to rest in the sanctuary with all

due pomp and magnificence, Solomon called all the masters together and said: 'My brothers, the traitors who committed this murder must not go unpunished. Their identity can be discovered, this is why I command you to carry out a search with all the ardour and care possible. And when they are discovered, I wish no harm to befall them; they should be brought to me alive so that whatever vengeance is undertaken, it will be mine. To this effect, then, I command twenty-seven of you to carry out this search, taking care to obey my orders exactly.' Each of them wished to be included, but Solomon, always just and moderate in his desires, repeated that only twenty-seven were needed and that nine would take the eastern road, nine the southern road, and the others the western road, and that they would all be armed with cudgels against whatever dangers they might encounter. He had them named directly, by general vote, and those who were chosen left immediately, promising to carry out the king's orders to the letter.

The three traitors, Hiram's murderers, having resumed work following their crime, and seeing that Hiram's body had been discovered, felt certain that Solomon would proceed to an investigation in order to determine who the killers were, which is precisely what did occur. They left Jerusalem at nightfall, splitting up so that were they to be discovered, they would be less suspect. Each fled, going far from Jerusalem and hiding in foreign lands.

The fourth day of walking was scarcely over when nine of the masters found themselves, utterly fatigued, surrounded by the rocks of a valley at the foot of the Lebanon Mountains. They rested there, and as night was falling, one of them stood guard somewhat ahead of the others. The watch he was keeping caused him to walk some distance away and he perceived a far-off tiny light, gleaming through a crack in the rock. He was surprised and he trembled, but at last took courage and ran to the spot, resolved to find out what it was. As soon as he drew near, a cold sweat broke out all over his body, but at last he again took courage and made ready to enter what had turned out to be the entrance of a cave from which the light was shining. The entrance was narrow and very low so that he had to bend over, his right hand extended before his head as protection against the points of rock, placing one foot ahead of the other, making as little noise as possible. In this way, he came finally to the heart of the cave where he saw a man lying asleep. He recognized him immediately as one of the workers at the temple site in Jerusalem, one of the class of fellows, and certain that he had come upon one of the assassins, his desire to avenge the death of Hiram made him forget Solomon's commands, and arming himself with a dagger which he found lying at the traitor's feet, he plunged it into his body, then cut off his head. Having done this, he felt himself suddenly thirsty, then seeing a spring that bubbled at the traitor's feet, he quenched his thirst before leaving the cave, the dagger in one hand, the head of the traitor in the other, holding it by the hair.

In this way he rejoined his comrades, who were seized with horror at the sight. He told what had occurred in the cave and how he had come upon the traitor who had sought refuge there. But his comrades explained to him that his too-great zeal had caused him to disobey the orders of the king. Realizing his fault, he stood speechless, but his comrades, familiar with the goodness and mercy of the king, promised him to obtain his pardon. They immediately took the road back to Jerusalem, accompanied by he who still held the traitor's head in one hand and the dagger in the other. They arrived nine days after their initial departure, at the moment when Solomon, as was his custom, had closed himself in the sanctuary with the masters to mourn for the good and worthy master Hiram. All nine went in, that is, eight together, and the ninth brandishing the head and the dagger and crying three times, 'mecum', which means *vengeance*, making a genuflexion at each cry. But Solomon trembled at the sight and said: 'Wretch, what have you done? Did I not tell you that all vengeance was to be mine?'

Immediately all the masters placed one knee on the ground and cried: 'Be merciful to him!' explaining that it was his too-great zeal alone which had caused him to forget his orders. Full of kindness, Solomon pardoned him and ordered that the traitor's head be exposed on the end of an iron pole at one of the doors of the temple, in full sight of all the workers. This was immediately carried out, and attention was directed to the discovery of the two remaining traitors.

Third Legend

Seeing that the traitors had split up, Solomon believed it would be difficult to find the two others, and so he had an edict published throught his kingdom, prohibiting anyone from opening his door to a stranger and promising huge rewards to those who might bring the traitors to Jerusalem or give knowledge of their whereabouts. A worker in the quarries of Tyre was well acquainted with a foreign man who had taken refuge in a cave near the quarries and who had confided his secret, making the worker promise to guard it with his life. Since this man came daily to the next village in order to procure food for the fugitive in the cave, he found himself therein at precisely the moment that Solomon's edict was made known and thought long about the rewards promised to those who would assist in the discovery of Hiram's murderers. Personal interest eventually won out over fidelity to the promise he had made. Thereupon he left, taking the road to Jerusalem.

Soon he met up with nine masters, deputized to search for the guilty ones, and seeing that their presence made him change colour, these men asked him where he came from and where he was going. He made a gesture as if to tear out his tongue, placed one knee on the ground and kissing the right hand of his interlocutor, said: 'I believe you to be the envoys of Solomon, seeking the traitors who murdered the architect of the temple. I have something to say, although I promised to keep silence. I cannot do otherwise than to follow the orders of king Solomon which he has made known to us in an edict. One of the traitors you seek is a day's walk from here, hiding in a cave among the rocks near the quarries of Tyre and next to a large bush. A dog is stationed at the entrance of the cave in order to warn of anyone's approach.'

Hearing this, the masters commanded him to lead them to this cave. He obeyed and took them to the quarries of Tyre, pointing out the place where the traitor lay in hiding. They had been gone from Jerusalem fourteen days when they discovered the traitor. Night was falling, the sky was overcast and a rainbow had formed above the bush, making it seem to burn. As they stared, they became aware of the entrance of the cave. They drew closer, saw the dog asleep, and took off their shoes so as not to be heard by him. A few of them went into the cave where they found the traitor asleep. They bound him and led him back to Jerusalem along with the man who had taken them to him.

They arrived on the eighteenth day following their departure just at the time when work on the temple was ceasing. Solomon and all the masters were in the sanctuary, mourning Hiram as was their custom. The nine went in, presenting the traitor to Solomon, who questioned him and made him admit his guilt. Solomon passed sentence that his body be laid open, his heart torn out, his head cut off and placed on the end of a metal bar, like the first, in full view of the workers. And his body was thrown on a rubbish heap to serve as fodder for scavengers. Solomon then rewarded the quarry worker and sent him, satisfied, back to his country. And attention turned to the search for the third and final traitor.

Fourth Legend

The last nine masters had begun to despair of ever finding the third traitor when on the twenty-second day of their search they found themselves lost in a forest of Lebanon and obliged to cross over several perilous places. They had to spend the night there; they naturally chose spots where they could rest assured of protection from the wild beasts that roamed the countryside. The next morning as day was beginning to break, one of them set out to explore a little this place in which they were. From a distance he spied a man with an axe who lay at the foot of a rock. It was the traitor they were looking for, who, having learned of the arrest of his accomplices, was fleeing into the desert to hide. Seeing one of the masters coming towards him and recognizing him from the site of the temple in Jerusalem, he got up and came forward, thinking he had nothing to fear from a single man. But then noticing the eight others further off, he turned and fled with all his strength, all of which only served to prove his guilt to the masters, indicating he was, in fact, the one they were seeking.

They gave pursuit. At last the traitor, fatigued by the difficult terrain he was obliged to cross, could do nothing more than wait for them resolutely, determined to defend himself and die rather than be taken. As he was armed with an axe, he threatened to spare none of them. Paying no attention, the masters, armed with their cudgels, drew closer to him, telling him to give himself up. But stubborn in his resolve, he jumped into the midst of them and defended himself furiously for a long time, without wounding any of them, for the masters only warded off his blows, wishing to bring him back alive to Solomon in Jerusalem. And to this end, half of them rested while the others fought.

Night was beginning to fall when the masters, fearful lest the darkness allow the traitor's escape, attacked him in

full force, seizing him at the very moment he wished to
jump from the edge of a high rock. Then they disarmed
him, bound him and led him back to Jerusalem where they
arrived on the twenty-seventh day following their departure, at that same time of day when Solomon and the
other masters were in the sanctuary, praying to the Eternal
and mourning Hiram. The returning masters went in and
presented the traitor to Solomon, who questioned him and
found he was unable to justify himself. He was condemned
to have his stomach opened, his entrails torn out, his head
cut off and the remainder of his body burned and the
ashes scattered to the four corners of the earth. His head
was exposed on the end of an iron bar. The names of the
traitors were written out and hung from each pole, with
tools like those they had used in the murder of Hiram. All
three were of the tribe of Judah: the oldest was named
Sebal, the second, Oterlut, and the third, Stokin. For three
days the three heads remained in sight of all the workers
on the temple. The third day, Solomon had a great fire lit
and the three heads, the tools and the written names cast
into it where all was burned, entirely consumed. The ashes
were scattered to the four corners of the earth.

All these things being accomplished, Solomon directed
the work on the temple with the aid of all the masters, and
peace was restored.

History of the Knight of the Lion

It is said that when Solomon had pardoned the fellows
who had considered revolt and had made certain they had
returned to their duties, one of these same fellows who
could not forget the punishment meted out to his three
companions and finding it unjust, resolved himself to make
an attempt on the life of Solomon. He entered his palace
with a dagger and killed one of the king's officers who
tried to stop him. He then fought with Solomon who

forced him to take flight and to flee to a hiding place in the mountains. Solomon's guards spent twelve days in pursuit of him with no success, when one of them named Boece saw a lion dragging a man into its lair. He fought with the lion and killed it and recognized the man as he whom they were seeking, choked to death by the lion. Boece cut off his head and carried it to Solomon, who rewarded him by giving him a ribbon, symbol of virtue, from which hung a golden lion, symbol of valour; and in its mouth the lion held the cudgel with which it had been killed.

After the temple was finished, several workers placed themselves under a single leader and worked for the reformation of moral behaviour, building spiritual edifices and gaining a reputation for their charity. They were called the Kadosh Fathers, which means 'detached by the holiness of their lives'.

They did not last too long a time, however, for they forgot their duty and their obligations, and avarice made them hypocrites.

The Ptolemy Philadelphians, kings of Egypt, princes of astrologers, were among the most celebrated and constant friends of truth; they ordered that sixty brothers work on a translation of the holy Scriptures.

The Kadosh Fathers soon strayed from their duties by over-reaching the limits of decency. Nevertheless, the order was preserved, for several of them, devoted observers of the laws they had originated, withdrew to themselves. They elected a grand master for life; one part remained in Syria and Sicily, centring their lives on good works; the other part went to live in the lands which they held in Lybia and Thebaid. These same solitary places were later inhabited by recluses known as Fathers of the Desert; once again they were called Kadosh, meaning 'holy' or 'separate'.

Neither Jews nor Christians have ever said anything bad of them. Their grand master was named Manchemm.

After the destruction of the temple, several embraced Christianity, adopting it because they saw nothing in it which was not in conformity to their way. They formed groups, members of a single larger family. All they possessed became common property. Alexander, patriarch of Alexandria, was the movement's greatest partisan and ornament. They passed their lives praising and blessing God and helping the poor whom they considered their own brothers. It is in this way that this respectable order maintained itself until near the end of the sixth century; and all brothers today seek to enhance its honoured reputation.

The Key to the Masonic Parables

Solomon is the personification of supreme knowledge and wisdom.

The temple is the realization and image of the hierarchic reign of truth and reason on the earth.

Hiram is man, come to power through knowledge and wisdom.

He governs with reason and order, giving to each according to his works.

Each degree of the order has a word which expresses its capacity for understanding.

There is only one word for Hiram; but this word can be pronounced in three different ways.

One way is for the apprentices;

And pronounced by them it signifies — nature,

And is explained through work.

Another way is for the fellows,

And with them it signifies — thought, explained through study.

Still another way is for the masters; and, in their mouths, the word signifies truth and is explained through wisdom.

There are three degrees in the hierarchy of beings;
There are three gates to the temple;
There are three rays in a beam of light;
There are three forces in nature.

These forces are symbolized by the measuring stick which unites, by the metal rod or lever which elevates, and the mallet which steadies and makes firm.

The rebellion of brute instinct against the autocracy of wisdom arms itself successively with these three forces.

There are three rebels:
The rebel against nature,
The rebel against knowledge,
The rebel against truth.

They were symbolized in the hell of the ancients by the three heads of Cerberus.

In the Bible they are symbolized by Corea, Dathan and Abiron.

In Masonic legend they are designated by symbols whose Qabalistic combinations vary according to the degree of initiation.

The first, ordinarily called Abiram or murderer of Hiram, strikes the grand master with the measuring stick.

It is in this way that so many of the just were sacrificed in the name of the law.

The second, named Miphiboseth, from the name of an absurd pretender to David's throne, strikes Hiram with the iron rod.

It is thus that popular reaction to tyranny becomes another tyranny and proves even deadlier to the reign of wisdom and virtue.

Finally, the third puts an end to Hiram with the mallet, as do the brutal restorers of so-called order, who ensure their authority by crushing and oppressing intelligence.

The acacia branch on Hiram's grave is like the cross on the altars of Christ.

This is the symbol of knowledge which survives knowledge itself and which for ever protests against the murderers of thought.

When man's errors have disturbed the order of things, nature intervenes, like Solomon in the temple.

The death of Hiram must always be avenged, the murderers may go unpunished for a while, but their time will come.

He who struck with the measuring stick provoked the dagger's blow.

He who struck with the iron rod will die by the axe.

He who was momentarily victorious with the mallet will fall victim to the force he misused and will be choked by the lion.

The murderer of the measuring stick is unmasked by the very lamp which gives him light and by the spring where he quenches his own thirst, that is, he cannot escape retaliation.

The murderer of the iron bar will be taken by surprise when his watchfulness fails, like that of a sleeping dog.

The lion who devours the murderer of the mallet is one of the forms of the Sphinx of Oedipus; and he who conquers him deserves to succeed Hiram.

The putrified body of Hiram shows that dead, exhausted forms are not resurrected. Hiram is the only true, the only legitimate king of the world, and it is of him one should speak in saying:

The king is dead!

Long live the king!

Freemasonry has as its goal the reconstitution of Hiram's monarchy,

And the spiritual rebuilding of the temple.

Then the three-headed dragon will be bound in chains,

Then the shadows of the three murderers will be confined to darkness.

Then the living stone, the cubic stone, the golden cube, the cube with twelve doors, the new Jerusalem will come down to earth from heaven, according to the Qabalistic prophecy of St John.

The spring, flowing near the first murderer, shows that the rebellion of the first age was punished by the flood.

The burning bush and rainbow which lead to the discovery of the second murderer represent the holy Qabalah which rises in opposition to the hypocritical, idolatrous dogmas of the second age.

Finally, the vanquished lion represents the triumph of mind over matter and the submission of brute force to intelligence, which is to be a sign of consummation and of the coming of the *sanctum regnum*.

Since the beginning, by creative mind, of work on the building of the temple of truth, Hiram has been killed many times, and always resurrected.

Hiram is Adonis killed by the bear,

He is Osiris, murdered by Set,

He is Pythagorus outlawed,

He is Orpheus torn to pieces by the Bacchantes,

He is Moses, buried, alive perhaps, in the caves of Mount Nebo,

He is Jesus, murdered by three traitors, Caiphus, Judas Iscariot and Pilate,

He is Jacques de Molay, condemned by a Pope, denounced by a false brother, and burned by order of a king.

The work of the temple is that of Messianism, that is, the accomplishment of Israelite and Christian symbolism.

It is order maintained through the equilibrium of duty and right, unshakeable foundations of power.

It is the re-establishment of the hierarchic initiation and of the ministry of thought, ruling the monarchy of strength and intelligence.

Everything that is done in the world would lack meaning if this work were not some day accomplished.

The Story of Phaleg

When all men were gathered together on the plain of Sennar, under the reign of Nimrod, there was a great architect named Phaleg.

He was the son of Eber, father of the Hebrews, and to protect mankind from a new flood, he drew the plan of a tower.

The first section of the tower was to be round, having twelve doors and seventy-two pillars.

The second was to be square with nine storeys, the third, a triangular spiral with forty-two turns.

The fourth was to be cylindrical with seventy-two storeys.

Seven staircases joined each of the storeys to the others.

The doors of each storey were to be opened and closed by means of mechanisms whose functioning was to be guarded as a hierarchic secret.

All inhabitants of the tower were to have equal civil rights, for those at the top could not live without the assistance of those at the bottom, and those below could not protect themselves from surprise attack without the vigilance of those above.

Such was the plan of Phaleg.

But the workers were disloyal to the great architect.

Secrets from above were revealed to those who worked below, the doors would no longer close, some tried to barricade them, others forced an entry in order to regain the safety of the heights.

And in addition, all wished to work as they liked, without consulting the plans of Phaleg.

Confusion sprang up in their language as it did in their work, and part of the tower collapsed while the rest remained unfinished, for the workers refused to aid one another.

And confusion reigned in their language for there was no more unity in their thought.

Phaleg then understood that he had hoped for too much from men in thinking they would understand one another.

But these men transferred the fault to him and denounced him to Nimrod.

Nimrod condemned him to death.

Phaleg disappeared and it was not known what happened to him.

Nimrod believed he had had him killed and he erected an idol to which he gave the name Phaleg and which gave out oracles in favour of Nimrod's tyranny. But in reality Phaleg had fled into the desert.

He made a trip round the known world as expiation for the too generous error he had committed.

And everywhere he stopped, he built a triangular tabernacle.

One of these monuments was rediscovered in Prussia in 553 in the digs of a salt mine.

Fifteen cubits below ground level a triangular building was found; inside it there was a white marble column on whose base the entire story was written in Hebrew.

Beside this column a tombstone was discovered, covered with dust, but under which lay an agate panel bearing the following epitaph:

Here lie the ashes of our G∴A∴ of the Tower of Babel . . .

Adonai has forgiven him the sins of men, for he loved them.

In humiliation he died for them, and thus he has paid for the magnificence of the idols of Nimrod.

The Crossing of the River Nabuzanai

In the seventieth year of the captivity of the Israelites in Babylon, King Cyrus, lying in his bed in the palace, had a dream which troubled him.

He saw a dove hovering above his head and a terrible lion coming towards him.

And as he sought for a means to escape the lion's ferocity, he heard the dove say: 'Give the captives their freedom.'

The king arose, heavy with thought, and was told that a wise Israelite, born on the other side of the river Nabuzanai, had asked to speak with the king.

The king bid this wise man enter, and having recounted the dream he had had, he asked for its interpretation.

Zorobabel (for such was the Israelite's name) said to the king that the Jews must be sent back to their own land and the temple of God rebuilt.

'Oh, king!' said he. 'To hold a people captive by force is to misuse force, itself.

'Force is the lion you saw in your dream. He must be conquered by justice.

'The dove is understanding and mercy and light.'

Cyrus said to him: 'Go, then, assemble all your brothers and rebuild the temple of God.'

Then he gave him a sword, a trowel and a key.

He also gathered together the spoils of the temple which had been pillaged by his predecessors and gave them to Zorobabel.

Then the Israelites came together and made ready to cross the river Nabuzanai.

The first to set foot in the water were devoured by monsters who came out of the deep.

Others arrived and saw that the river bore a hideous collection of bones and other debris.

Now, the monsters who had devoured these victims were a crocodile and a serpent.

The crocodile wore a gold crown on his head; the serpent, a diadem.

It was the evil spirits of the river, the water-demons who, under a thousand frightening forms, offered them all the men who attempted to cross to the other side.

When these things were reported to Zorobabel, he had large fires built on the river banks. Then he had a floating bridge constructed and cast in the middle of the waters.

Thus the bridge found its way on to the river without the demons being aware of its construction, for their attention was occupied elsewhere, being attracted by the fires on the banks.

The people of Israel crossed over.

On the bridge were traced three magic letters which served as talismans for the captives returning to their land.

These were the letters L∴ D∴ P∴

They stood for the cross, the angular stone and the Word of Truth.

The cross is an expression of creation and sacrifice.

The angular stone is the foundation of the temple, and the Word of Truth presides over the acts of all workers.

The angular stone is called Kether; the cross is Chokmah, and the Word of life is named Binah.

It was by means of these signs that the deliverance of Israel was to be accomplished.

These three letters can be combined in three ways:

These are the signs of the nine masters who avenged the death of Hiram.

These are the hieroglyphs of the three grades of Freemasonry.

In modern terms they signify: Liberty, duty, power.

And Qabalistically they are written thus:

P

L   D

Or: power upheld by duty and liberty.

For the vulgar, these letters mean: liberty of passage.

For apprentices and fellows, they mean: liberty of thought.

Baphomet

Tem.˙. o.˙. h.˙. p.˙. Abb.˙.

Binario Verbum Vitae Mortem
et Vitam Aequilibrans

Several figures of Baphomet* exist.

Sometimes he is shown with a beard, the horns of a male goat, the face of a man, the breast of a woman, the mane and claws of a lion, the wings of an eagle and the hooves of a bull.

His is the resurrected sphinx of Thebes, Oedipus's monster, by turns captive and conqueror.

He is knowledge rising in opposition to idolatry, protesting through the very monstrosity of the idol.

Between his horns he carries the torch of life, and the living soul of this torch is God.

The Israelites were forbidden to give divine concepts the figure of man or of any animal; thus, on the ark of the covenant and in the sanctuary, they dared sculpt only cherubs, that is, sphinxes with the bodies of bulls and the heads of men, eagles or lions.

These mixed figures reproduced neither the complete form of man, nor that of any animal.

These hybrid creations of impossible animals gave to understand that the image was not an idol or reproduction of a living thing, but rather a character or representation of something having its existence in thought.

Baphomet is not worshipped; it is God who is worshipped, the faceless God behind this formless form, this image which resembles no created being.

Baphomet is not a God: he is the sign of initiation. He is also the hieroglyphic figure of the great divine Tetragrammaton.

He is a hold-over from the Cherbus of the ark and the

* For the figure of Baphomet, see *Dogma and Ritual of High Magic*, II.

Holy of holies.

He is the guardian of the key to the temple.

Baphomet is analogous to the dark God of Rabbi Simeon.

He is the dark side of the divine face. This is why, during initiation ceremonies, the member elect must kiss the hind-face of Baphomet or, to give him a more vulgar name, the Devil. Now, in the symbolism of the two faces, the hind-face of God is the Devil and the hind-face of the Devil is the hieroglyphic face of God.

Why the name of Freemasons? Free from what? From the fear of God? Yes, doubtless, for when one fears God, one is looking at him from behind. The dreadful God is the black God, the Devil. The Freemasons wish to build a spiritual temple to the one God, the God of light, the God of understanding and philanthropy. They oppose the God of the Devil and the Devil of God. But they respect the pious beliefs of Socrates, of Vincent de Paul and of Fenelon. What they would willingly, with Voltaire, call the 'vile infamy' is this face, or better, this foolishness which during the Middle Ages took the place of God.

The brighter the light, the darker its bordering shadow. Christianity is at the same time the salvation and the scourge of the world. It is the most sublime of wisdoms and the most frightening of follies. If Jesus was not God, he was the most dangerous of evil-doers. The Jesus of Veuillot is execrable. Renan's is inexcusable. The Gospels' is unexplainable, but the Jesus of Vincent de Paul and of Fenelon is lovable and can be worshipped. If Christianity is for you the condemnation of reason, the despotism of ignorance and of the majority of mankind, you are the enemy of humanity. But if by Christianity you mean the life of God in humanity, the heroism of philanthropy, the reign of charity which gives divinity to the sacrifices of men and through communion makes them live the same life, inspired with the same love, then you are a saviour of the world.

The religion of Moses is a truth; the so-called Mosaic religion of the Pharisees was a lie.

The religion of Jesus is the same truth, having progressed a step forward, revealing itself to man in a new manifestation. The religion of the inquisitors and oppressors of human consciousness is a lie.

The Catholicism of the Church Fathers and the saints is a truth. The Catholicism of Veuillot is a lie.

It is this lie that Freemasonry has taken upon itself to combat in favour of truth.

Freemasonry wants nothing to do with the doctrines of men like Torquemada and Escobar, but it does admit among its symbols those of Hermes, Moses and Jesus Christ. The pelican at the foot of the cross is embroidered on the ribbon of its initiates of the highest grade. It excludes only fanaticism, ignorance, foolish credulity, and hate; but it believes in one dogma, single in spirit though multiple in form, that of humanity. Its religion is not Judaism, enemy of all other peoples, nor exclusive Catholicism, nor strict Protestantism, but true catholicity worthy of this name, that is, universal philanthropy! This is the Messianism of the Hebrews!

Everything is true in the books of Hermes. But attempts to keep them from the profane have rendered them useless, so to speak, to the world.

Everything is true in the dogma of Moses; what is false is the exclusivity and despotism of some rabbis. Everything is true in the Christian dogma; but Catholic priests have committed the same faults as the rabbis of Judaism.

These dogmas complete and explain one another and their synthesis will be the religion of the future.

The error of the disciples of Hermes was this: error must be left to the profane and truth should be rendered impenetrable to everyone, except priest and kings.

Idolatry, despotism and attempts to destroy the priesthood were the bitter fruits of this doctrine.

The error of the Jews was to claim to be a unique and

privileged nation, all other peoples being accursed and they alone being God's elect.

And the Jews, victims of a cruel twist of fate, have been cursed and persecuted by all other nations.

The Catholics have been deceived by three fundamental errors:

1. They believed that faith must at all costs be imposed on reason and even on science, whose progress they have combated.

2. They attributed to the Pope an infallibility which was not only conservative and disciplinary, but absolute, like that of God.

3. They thought that man should revile himself, deny his own importance and make himself unhappy as a preparation for the life to come; whereas quite the contrary is true. Man should cultivate all his faculties, develop them, fill out his soul, learn, know and love his life, in a word: be happy. For this present life is in fact a preparation for the future life and man's eternal happiness begins only when he has acquired the profound peace which results from perfect balance.

These errors have caused nature, science and reason to protest against them, thereby making it momentarily appear that all faith has been lost and all religion fled from the face of the earth.

But the world could no more survive without religion than man could live without a heart. When all religions are dead, the unique and universal religion will live on. This will occur when there is one accord among all men in their belief in universal solidarity, unity of aspiration, diversity of expression, faith in a single God, freedom for symbolism and tolerance of images, orthodoxy in charity, with universality always at the heart of all and, not to say indifference, deference to the spirit, analogous in all peoples, working variously among them, the perfectability of dogma, the possible amelioration of cults, but still behind all this the great and unchanging faith of Israel in one single God at once immaterial, immutable and insubstantial, all of whose conventional representations are idols, a faith in reason, the universal law and in the existence of one nation alone, the instrument of God for the creation and conservation of both insects and galaxies!

And it is also under Israel's auspices and by means of its commercial influence that we hope to see established on earth:

The association of all financial interests;

The federation of peoples;

The alliance of all religious cults;

And universal solidarity.

Profession of Faith*

We believe in the eternal and infinite sovereignty of unchanging wisdom and creative intelligence.

We believe in the supreme beauty of equitable goodness and merciful, loving justice.

We believe in the productivity of progress within order and in an order which is eternally progressing.

We believe in the principle of universal life, in the principle of Being and beings for ever distinct from Being and beings, but necessarily present within Being and within beings.

We believe that the entire principle, within everything and everywhere, cannot be contained, enclosed, limited, determined or defined in any way, and that as a consequence, any form, any special name, any personal exclusive revelation of this principle is idolatry and error.

We believe that principle resides in all of us and speaks to each one of us through the voice of consciousness;

* These pages are taken from the Letters of Eliphas Lévi which Monsieur le Baron de Spedadieri has kindly transmitted to us. They are unpublished and we believe our readers will welcome these extracts; we hope later to publish the letters themselves *in extenso*.
Editor's Note

That consciousness cannot be enlightened without the participation of faith, of reason, of science and of spirituality.

We believe in absolute reason which must guide and correct particular reasonings, which must be the basis for faith and the standard for all dogmas, lest there be fanaticism, folly and error.

We believe in absolute love which is called charity and inspires sacrifice.

We believe that, in order to grow, one must give, that one is happy as a result of others' happiness, and that well-regulated egoism must begin with one's neighbour.

We believe in liberty, in absolute independence, even in the royalty of self, the relative divinity of the human will when it is governed by sovereign reason.

We believe that God himself – the great undefinable principle – can be neither the despotic ruler nor the executioner-judge of his creatures; that he can neither reward nor punish them, but that the law carries within itself its own consequence, so that good is of itself the reward for good and evil, the punishment but also the remedy, for evil.

We believe that the spirit of charity alone is inflexible when it inspires devotion and peace, but that all men can fall prey to error, above all when acting on things they do not know and so do not comprehend.

We believe in the catholicity, that is, universality, of dogma.

We believe that in religion all intelligent men accept the same truths and only disagree regarding errors.

We believe that the most reasonable men are also the most patient, and that the persecutors of those whose beliefs differ prove by the very violence of their persecution that they are in error.

We believe that all gods are phantoms and that all idols are nothing; that established faiths should make place for others, and that the wise man can prey in a mosque or church indifferently. However we prefer the mosque to the pagoda and the church to the mosque, provided that the church remain unsullied by the presence of a bad priest.

In a word, we believe in a single God and in a single religion. In God blessing all gods and in religion absorbing or annihilating all religions.

We believe in universal, absolute and infinite being, demonstrated by the impossibility of nothingness, and we do not accept that nothing can exist, nor that it can become something.

We recognize in Being two essential modes of existence, idea and form, intelligence and action.

We believe in truth, which is Being conceived by Idea;

In reality, which is Idea demonstrated or capable of demonstration by science;

In Justice, which is Being put into action in accordance with its true nature and reasonable proportions.

We believe in the perpetual, progressive revelation of God in the developments of our intelligence and of our love.

We believe in the spirit of truth as inseparable from the spirit of charity, and we refer to this, along with the Catholic Church, as:

'The spirit of science opposed to the obscurantism of bad priests;

'The spirit of intelligence opposed to the foolishness of superstition;

'The spirit of force to withstand the prejudices and calumny of false believers;

'The spirit of piety, filial, social or humanitarian, opposed to the impious egoism of those who would let all else perish in order to save their souls;

'The spirit of wise counsel, for true charity begins with the spirit and brings its first assistance to the soul;'

And finally, 'The spirit of the fear of evil, which tramples down the fear of men and teaches us not to render unto evil a sacrilegious cult based on a capricious and wicked God.'

We believe that this Spirit is that of the Gospels and of Jesus Christ.

This is why we worship the living, acting God in Jesus Christ, without making him a distinct God, separable from God, himself. For Jesus was a true man and completely human, as we are, but sanctified by the plenitude of the divine Spirit speaking through his mouth, living and acting through him.

We believe in the moral and divine sense of the legendary Gospels whose letter is imperfect, but whose spirit is eternal.

We believe the laws of Moses, of the Apostles and of their successors, the Popes, to have been transitory, but that the law of charity is eternal.

This.is why we reject and condemn no one.

We believe that well-ordered egoism begins with others and the truly rich are those who give.

We believe in the infallibility of the spirit of charity, and not in the dogmatic temerity of a few men.

We believe in the eternal life. Thus we do not fear death for ourselves or for those we love.

We ascribe integrally to the thirteen articles of the Symbol of Maimonides, and as a consequence we regard the Israelites as our brothers.

We believe that God alone is God, and that Mohammed was one of *precursory words* (which is what the word *prophet* signifies), and we are sympathetic to the Muslims.

But we both pity and blame the Jews for calling us *goy* and the Muslims for calling us *giaours*. In this we cannot be in sympathy with them, for in this they are outside the bounds of charity.

We ascribe to the Symbol of the Apostles, of St Athanasius and of Nicaea, recognizing, however, that they must be explained in a hierarchical manner and that they express the highest mysteries of occult philosophy.

But we reprove reprobation and we excommunicate

excommunication as offences against charity and universal solidarity.

We admit the arbitral and disciplinary infallibility of the head of the Church, but we consider it foolish to ascribe to him an arbitrary infallibility in the creation of dogma.

The Pope is the legal interpreter and preserver of ancient beliefs; but should he wish to impose new ones, he strays from his path of duty and has no more authority than any other speaker of foolishness.

We study tradition, but we do not judge it a critical authority, for it is the common receptacle of antiquity's errors as well as its truths.

Such is the profession of faith which should unite and slowly absorb all others. Such is the religion of great souls to come. How many men are presently capable of understanding it? I cannot say; but I think that if a prophet were to speak of it aloud before all assembled peoples, he would be stoned by the priests, disdained by the people and briefly regretted by a few wise men.

In the meantime, the Pope raises troops and invents dogma. Veuillot distills his gall and analyses the smells of Paris. In its turn, Paris holds its nose against the smell of Veuillot. Veuillot washes his hands of it all and says: this is only the perfume of Rome!

And temporal sovereignty, the Vatican's prostitute, does not blush at having Veuillot for her souteneur!

In Paris, censorship forbids the representation of Ponsard's *Galilée*. Truly, has the world come to an end?

Oh, reign of fear for ever reborn, continual revolt of beast against angel, inevitable alliance of tyrannies against intelligence however free, licensed stupidity, condemned spirit, how long will you continue to hold this poor world upside down?

Eliphas Lévi

Elements of the Qabalah
in Ten Lessons
Letters of Eliphas Lévi*

First Lesson
GENERAL PROLEGOMENA

Friend and Brother,

I can give you this title because you are searching for the truth in the sincerity of your heart, ready to make the necessary sacrifices in order to find it.

Truth, being the essence of all that is, is not difficult to find: it is within us and we are within it. It is like light and the blind do not see it.

Being is. This is incontestable and absolute. The exact idea of Being is truth; its knowledge is science; its ideal expression is reason; its activity is creation and justice.

You wish to believe, you say. For this, it is enough to know and to love truth. For the true faith is the unshakeable adhesion of the mind to the necessary deductions of science in conjectural infinity.

Only occult sciences give certitude, for they have their bases in realities and not in dreams.

In every religious symbol, they bring out the true and the false. What is true is the same everywhere, but falsehoods spring up according to places, times and people.

These sciences are three: the Qabalah, Magic and Hermeticism.

The Qabalah, or traditional science of the Hebrews, might be called the mathematics of human thought. It is the algebra of faith. It solves all problems of the soul as equations, by isolating the unknowns. It gives to ideas the

* These letters were kindly brought to our attention by a student of Eliphas Lévi, Monsieur Montaut. They appeared in the magazine, *Initiation* in 1891.

clarity and rigorous exactitude of numbers; its results, for the mind, are infallibility (always relative, however, to the sphere of human knowledge) and for the heart, profound peace.

Magic, or the science of the magi, has its ancient representatives in the disciples, and perhaps the teachers, of Zoroaster. It is the knowledge of secret and particular laws of nature which produce hidden forces, magnets and loadstones which may exist even outside the realm of metal. In a word, and to use a modern expression, it is the science of universal magnetism.

Hermeticism is the science of nature hidden in the hieroglypics and symbols of the ancient world. It is the search for the principle of life, along with the dream (for those who have not yet achieved it) of accomplishing the great work, that is the reproduction by man of the divine, natural fire which creates and recreates beings.

Here, my friend, are the things you desire to study. The circle they enclose is immense, but the principles are so simple that they are represented and contained in the signs of the numbers and in the letters of the alphabet. 'It is a labour of Hercules that is also a child's game,' say the masters of holy science.

Characteristics necessary to success in this study are a great rectitude of judgment and a great independence of mind. One must rid oneself of all prejudice and every preconceived notion, and it is for this reason that Christ said: 'Unless you become as a little child, you cannot enter the Malkouht,' that is, the kingdom of knowledge.

We will begin with the Qabalah, whose divisions are these: Berechith, Mercavah, Gematria and Lemurah.

Yours in the holy science,
Eliphas Lévi

Second Lesson
The Qabalah — Goal and Method

In studying the Qabalah, one should strive to arrive at profound peace by means of tranquillity of mind and peace of heart.

Tranquillity of mind is an effect of certainty; peace of heart comes from patience and faith.

Without faith, science leads to doubt; without science, faith leads to superstition. Uniting them brings certainty, but in so doing they must never be confused with each other. The object of faith is hypothesis, and this becomes certitude when the hypothesis is necessitated by evidence or by the demonstrations of science.

Science establishes facts. From the repetition of facts, it presupposes laws. The generality of facts in the presence of such and such a force demonstrates the existence of laws. Intelligent laws are necessarily imposed and governed by intelligence. Unity within the laws presupposes the unity of legislative intelligence. This intelligence, which we are forced to imagine, only seeing it at work in external manifestations, and which we can in no way define, is what we call God!

You receive my letter; there is an obvious fact. You recognize my handwriting and my thoughts and you conclude from this that it is indeed I who have written to you. This is a reasonable hypothesis, but the necessary hypothesis is that someone wrote the letter. It could be counterfeit, though you have no reason to suppose it is. Were you to suppose so, groundlessly, you would be making a very doubtful hypothesis. Were you to claim that the letter, fully written, fell from the sky, you would be making an absurd hypothesis.

Here is, then, according to Qabalistic method, how certitude is formed:

Evidence

Scientific demonstration	certitude
Necessary hypothesis	
Reasonable hypothesis	probability
Doubtful hypothesis	doubt
Absurd hypothesis	error

By keeping to this method, the mind acquires a veritable infallibility, for it affirms what it knows, believes what it must necessarily suppose, admits reasonable suppositions, examines doubtful ones, and rejects those which are absurd.

All the Qabalah is contained in what the masters call the thirty-two roads and the fifty gates.

The thirty-two roads are thirty-two absolute and real ideas attached to the signs of the ten arithmetical numbers and to the twenty-two letters of the Hebraic alphabet.

Here are these ideas:

NUMBERS

1	Supreme power	6	Beauty
2	Absolute wisdom	7	Victory
3	Infinite intelligence	8	Eternity
4	Goodness	9	Productivity
5	Justice or harshness	10	Reality

LETTERS

Aleph	Father	Lamed	Sacrifice
Beth	Mother	Mem	Death
Gimel	Nature	Nun	Reversibility
Daleth	Authority	Samekh	Universal being
He	Religion	Pe	Immortality
Vav	Liberty	Ayin	Balance
Zayin	Ownership	Sadhe	Shadow and reflection
Cheth	Distribution	Koph	Light
Teth	Prudence	Resh	Recognition
Yod	Order	Tav	Synthesis
Kaph	Force		

Third Lesson
Use of the Method

In the preceding lesson I spoke only of the thirty-two roads; later I will talk of the fifty gates.

The ideas expressed by numbers and letters are incontestable realities. These ideas follow from one another and agree like the numbers, themselves. One proceeds logically from one to the next. Man is the son of woman, but woman comes out of man as number comes out of unity. Woman clarifies nature, nature reveals authority, which creates religion, basis for liberty, which makes man master of himself and of the universe, etc . . . (Get hold of a Tarot — I believe in fact you already have one — and, in two series, lay out the ten allegorical cards numbered from one to twenty-one. You will see all the figures which correspond to the letters. As for the numbers from one to ten, you will find them repeated four times with the symbols of the baton or sceptre of the father, the cup or *délices* of the mother, the sword of love and the coins of productivity. The Tarot is included in the hieroglyphic book of the thirty-two roads, and its summary explanation can be found in the book attributed to the patriarch, Abraham, which is called *Sepher-Jezirah*.

The savant Court de Gebelin was the first to discover the importance of the Tarot, which is the great key to the hieratic hieroglyphs. Its symbols and numbers are to be found in the prophecies of Ezekiel and of St John. The Bible is an inspired book, but the Tarot is the book of inspiration. It has also been called the wheel, *rota*, whence *tarot* and *torah*. The ancient Rosicrucians knew it well and the Marquis de Suchet speaks of it in his book on visionaries.

It is from this book that our card games have come. Spanish cards still bear the principal signs of the primitive Tarot and they are used to play the game of the *hombre* or man, vague reminiscence of the early use of a mysterious book, containing oracular decrees about all human divinities.

The earliest Tarots were medals which have since become talismans. The *clavicules* or little keys of Solomon were made up of thirty-six talismans bearing seventy-two engravings analogous to the hieroglyphic figures of the Tarot. These figures, altered by copyists, can still be found on ancient *clavicules* which exist in some libraries. A manuscript of this type exists in the Bibliothèque Nationale and another in the Bibliothèque de l'Arsenal. The only authentic manuscripts of the *clavicules* are those which give the series of thirty-six talismans with the seventy-two mysterious names; the others, however ancient they may be, belong to fantasies of black magic and contain nothing more than clever tricks.

For an explanation of the Tarot, see my *Dogma and Ritual of True Magic*.

Yours in the holy science,
   Eliphas Lèvi

Fourth Lesson
The Qabalah I

Brother and Friend,

Bereschith means 'genesis'; Mercavah means 'chariot', alluding to the wheels and mysterious animals of Ezekiel.

The Bereschith and the Mercavah summarize the science of God and of the world.

I say 'science of God', and yet God is infinitely unknowable. His nature entirely escapes our investigations. He is the absolute principle of being and of beings and must not be confused with the effects he produces; and it can be said, affirming his existence all the while, that he is neither being nor a being. Such a definition confounds reason, without however causing us to go astray, and keeps us for ever from all idolatry.

God is the only absolute *postulatum* of all science, the entirely necessary hypothesis which serves as a basis for any certainty; and here is how our ancient masters established, above science itself, this assured hypothesis of faith: Being is. In Being is life. Life is made manifest by movement. Movement is perpetuated by the balancing of forces. Harmony results from the analogy of opposites. There are, in nature, an immutable law and an undefinable progress. A perpetual changing of forms and the indestructability of substance, this is what one finds upon observing the physical world.

Metaphysics presents us with analogous laws and facts either in an intellectual or a moral order, on one side, unchanging truth, on the other, fantasy and imagination. On one side there is goodness which is truth, on the other, evil, which is false, and from these apparent conflicts arise both judgment and virtue. Virtue is composed of goodness and justice. Its goodness makes it indulgent. Its justice makes it harsh. Good because it is just and just because it is good: it is always beautiful.

This great harmony of the physical and moral worlds, incapable of having a cause superior to itself, reveals and demonstrates to us the existence of an unchanging wisdom and of an infinitely active creative intelligence. Upon this wisdom and this intelligence, each inseparable from the other, reposes the supreme power which the Hebrews have named the crown. The crown and not the king, for the idea of a king would imply an idol. For Qabalists, the supreme power is the crown of the universe and the entirety of creation is the kingdom, or if you prefer, the domain of this crown.

No one can give what he has not, thus we can assume that what we see manifested in effects is also present in the cause.

God, then, is the supreme power or crown (Kether) which sits upon immutable wisdom (Chokmah) and creative intelligence (Binah); in him are goodness (Hesed) and justice (Geburah) which are the ideal of beauty (Tiphereth). In him are for ever victorious movement (Netzach) and the great eternal rest (Hod). His desire is a continual giving of life (Yesod) and his kingdom (Malkuth) is the immensity which populates the universe.

Enough: we are acquainted with God!

Yours in the holy science,

Eliphas Lévi

Fifth Lesson
The Qabalah II

Brother and Friend,

This rational conscience of divinity, spread over the ten ciphers which compose all numbers, give you the whole method of Qabalistic philosophy. This method is composed of thirty-two means or instruments of knowledge which are called the thirty-two roads, and of fifty subjects to which the science may be applied and that are called the fifty gates.

Universal synthetic science is thus regarded as a temple to which there lead thirty-two paths and which may be entered through thirty-two doors.

This numerical system, which could also be called decimal since it is based on the number ten, establishes by means of analogies an exact classification of all human knowledge. Nothing is more ingenious, but likewise nothing is more logical and exact.

This number ten applied to absolute notions of being in the divine order, in the metaphysical order and in the natural order is thus repeated three times which gives thirty for purposes of analysis; add syllepsis and synthesis, that is, unity which begins as a concept in the mind and unity which brings together as one all that is, and you have the thirty-two roads.

The fifty gates are a classification of all being into five series of ten each and which embraces all one can know and extends into the entire body of knowledge.

But it is not enough to have found an exact mathematical method; in order to be perfect, this method must be progressively revelatory, that is, it must give us the means of making all possible deductions unerringly, of obtaining new knowledge and of developing the mind without leaving anything to the capriciousness of the imagination.

This is what one obtains through the Gematria and the Lemurah, which are the mathematics of idea. The Qabalah has its ideal geometry, its philosophical algebra and its analogic trigonometry. It is thus that, so to speak, it obliges nature to render up her secrets.

Once such high knowledge is acquired, one goes on to the final revelations of the transcendental Qabalah, studying in the schememamphorash the source and reason of all dogmas.

There, brother and friend, is what there is for you to learn. Does it frighten you? My letters are short, but concise, and say much. I have spaced my first five lessons rather far apart so as to give you time for reflection. I can write to you more often if you so desire.

With the ardent wish of being useful to you, I remain, your devoted servant in the holy science,

Eliphas Lévi

Sixth Lesson
The Qabalah III

Brother and Friend,

The Bible gives man two names. The first is Adam, which means 'drawn from the earth' or 'man of earth'; the second is Enos or Enoch, which means 'divine man' or 'lifted to God'. According to Genesis it is Enos who first spoke publicly on the principle of beings and this same Enos was, it is said, taken alive up into heaven after having engraved the primitive elements of religion and universal science on two stones which are called the columns or pillars of Enoch.

This Enoch is not a person, but a personification of humanity uplifted by religion and science to a sense of immortality. At the time designated by the name of Enos or Enoch, the cult of God appears on earth and ritual worship begins. This time also marks the beginning of civilization with writing and the hieratic movements.

The civilizing genius which the Hebrews personify in Enoch was named Trismegistus by the Egyptians, and by the Greeks, Kadmos or Cadmus, he who saw the living stones of Thebes rise of themselves and take their place to the accompaniment of Amphion's lyre.

The primitive sacred book, the book that Postel calls the genesis of Enoch, is the first source of the Qabalah, tradition at once divine, human and religious. Here in all its simplicity appears the revelation of supreme intelligence to reason and to the love of man, the eternal law governing infinite expansion, the numbers in infinite expansion, the numbers in immensity and immensity in numbers, poetry in mathematics and mathematics in poetry.

Who would believe that the book which inspired all these theories and religious symbols has been preserved, coming down to us in the form of a deck of strange cards? Nothing is truer, however, and Court de Gebelin, since followed by all those who have seriously studied the symbolism of these cards, was the first to discover it, in the last century.

The alphabet and the ten numerical signs are of course the basic elements of all sciences. Add to them the signs of the four cardinal points of heaven or of the four seasons and you have the book of Enoch in its entirety. But each sign represents an absolute or, if you will, essential idea.

The form of each cipher and of each letter has its mathematical reason and hieroglyphic significance. Ideas, inseparable from numbers, follow their movement, by addition, multiplication, etc., and acquire their exactitude.

The book of Enoch is the arithmetic of thought.
   Yours in the holy science,
      Eliphas Lévi

Seventh Lesson
The Qabalah IV

Brother and Friend,
   In the twenty-two keys of the Tarot, Court de Gebelin saw the representation of Egyptian mysteries and attributed their invention to Hermes Trismegistus, who was also called Thoth. It is certain that the hieroglyphs of the Tarot can be found on the ancient monuments of Egypt; it is certain that the signs of this book, traced in synoptic ensembles on steles or metal tables similar to the Isiac table of Bembo, were separately reproduced on engraved stones or medals which later became amulets and talismans. Thus the pages of the infinite book were separated into diverse combinations in order to assemble, transpose and re-transpose them for the obtaining of inexhaustible oracles of truth.
   I have in my possession one of these ancient talismans which a travelling friend brought me from Egypt. It shows the two of coins, the figurative expression of the great law of polarity and equilibrium, producing harmony through the analogy of opposites. Here is how this symbol is shown in the Tarot which we possess and which is sold today. S The medallion I have is rather worn, about as big as a silver five-franc piece, but thicker. The two polaric points are shown exactly as in our Italian Tarot, a lotus flower with a halo.
   The astral current which separates and at the same time attracts the two polaric seats is represented on our Egyptian talisman by the Goat of Mendes placed between two vipers analogous to the serpents of the caduceus. On the reverse side, one sees an adept or Egyptian priest who, having substituted himself for Mendes between the two

points of universal equilibrium, is leading the goat, now simply a docile animal governed by man the imitator of God, down a long avenue planted with trees.

The ten numerical signs, the twenty-two letters of the alphabet and the four astronomical signs of the seasons are the summary of the entire Qabalah.

Twenty-two letters and ten numbers give the thirty-two ways of the Sepher Jetzirah; four gives the mercavah and the shememamphorash.

It is as simple as a child's game and as complicated as the most arduous problem of pure mathematics.

It is as profound and naïve as truth and nature.

These four elementary, astronomical signs are the four forms of the sphinx and the four animals of Ezekiel and St John.

Yours in the holy science,
    Eliphas Lévi

Eighth Lesson
The Qabalah V

Brother and Friend,

The science of the Qabalah makes doubt, as regards religion, impossible, for it alone reconciles reason with faith by showing that universal dogma, at bottom always and everywhere the same, though formulated differently in certain times and places, is the purest expression of the aspirations of the human mind, enlightened by a necessary faith. It points out the usefulness of religious practices which fortify will by fixing the attention, throwing light on all the cults. It proves that the most effective cult is that which brings together, so to speak, divinity and man, making him see it, touch it and incorporate it into himself. It is enough to say that I am speaking here of the Catholic religion.

This religion, to the vulgar mind, appears to be the most absurd of all, for it is the most *revealed*; I use the word in

its veritable sense, *revelare*, to re-veil, to veil again. You
know that, according to the Gospels, at the death of Christ
the veil of the temple was rent asunder, and all down the
ages the Church has worked dogmatically to weave a new
one.

It is true that the heads of the sanctuary, themselves,
having wished to become its princes, long ago lost the keys
of high initiation. This does not, however, prevent the
letter of dogma from being sacred, nor the sacraments from
having their effect. I have set forth in my books that the
Christian-Catholic cult is high magic organized and regula-
rized by symbolism and hierarchy. It is a safety device
offered to human weakness so as to fortify the desire for
good.

Nothing has been forgotten, neither the dark mysterious
temple, nor the incense, both calming and exalting, nor the
long monotonous chants which rock the brain into a kind
of semi-somnambulism. The dogma, whose obscure formulae appear to be the despair of all reason, serves as a
barrier to the quibblings of inexperienced and indiscreet
criticism. These formulae seem incomprehensible so as to
better represent infinity. The mass itself, celebrated in a
language which most of the people do not understand,
gives width to the thought of he who officiates and allows
him to satisfy, through prayer, all the needs of his mind
and heart. This is why the Catholic religion resembles this
sphinx of the fable who, century after century, becomes
its own successor, always arising from its ashes; this great
mystery of faith is simply a mystery of nature.

It would seem an enormous paradox were one to say
that the Catholic religion is the only one which can
justifiably be called natural, and yet, this is true, for it
alone satisfies with any fulness at all this natural need of
man, which is the religious sense.

Yours in the holy science,
   Eliphas Lévi

Ninth Lesson
The Qabalah VI

Brother and Friend,

If the Catholic-Christian dogma is entirely Qabalistic, the same must be said for the great religions of the ancient world. The legend of Krishna as it is recounted in the Bhagavadam, is a veritable Gospel, similar to ours, but more naïve, more brilliant. The incarnations of Vishnu number ten like the Sephiroth of the Qabalah and in some ways form a more complete revelation than ours. Osiris killed by Typhon, then resurrected by Isis, is Christ denied by the Jews, then honoured in the person of his mother. The *Thebaid* is a great religious epic which must be placed beside the great symbol of Prometheus. Antigone is as pure a type of divine woman as Mary. Everywhere good triumphs through voluntary sacrifice, after having been temporarily subjected to the wild assaults of evil. Even the rites are symbolic and are transmitted from one religion to another. Diadems, mitres, surplices belong to all the great religions. And so the conclusion is that all of them are false; whereas it is only this conclusion which is false. The truth is that religion, like humanity, is one, always progressing, always changing, always the same.

If, with the Egyptians, Jesus Christ is named Osiris, for the Scandinavians, Osiris is named Balder. He is killed by the wolf, Jeuris, but Odin calls him back to life, and the Valkyries themselves serve him hydromel in Valhalla. The skalds, the druids, the bards sing of the death and resurrection of Tarenis or of Tetenus, distribute to their faithful a sprig of holy mistletoe as we dispense the sacred palm during feasts of the summer solstice, and maintain a cult to virginity inspired by the priestesses of the isle of Seyne.

We can then, in all fair conscience, set about performing the duties imposed on us by our native religion. Religious practices are collective acts, repeated with direct, persevering intention. Such acts are always useful in that they strengthen the will, they are in a sense its gymnastics, and they bring us eventually to the spiritual goal which we wish to attain. Magic practices have the same end and give results analogous to religious practices, but less perfect.

How many men do not have the energy to do what they would like and what they ought to do? And there are such great numbers of women who devote themselves unflaggingly to labours as repugnant as those of the hospital or of teaching! Where do they find such strength? In small repeated religious practices. Each day they say their rosary, kneeling in prayer.

Yours in the holy science,
Eliphas Lévi

Tenth Lesson
The Qabalah VII

Brother and Friend,

Religion is not a servitude imposed on man, but an aid which has been offered him. From time immemorial, sacerdotal castes have sought to exploit, sell and transform this aid into an unbearable yoke and burden; and the evangelical work of Jesus had as its aim the separation of the priest from religion, or at least, the return of the priest to his place as the minister, the servant of religion, by giving back to human consciousness all its liberty and reason. Look at the parable of the Good Samaritan and at these precious words: the law was made for man and not man for the law. Woe to you who lay upon others burdens you would not so much as touch with the tip of your finger, etc. The official Church which declares itself infallible in the *Apocalypse*, the Qabalistic key to the Gospels, has always existed side by side with occult strains of Christianity that maintained an interpretation of dogma quite different from that given out to the vulgar.

The Templars, the Rosicrucians, the Freemasons of high grade, all belonged, before the French Revolution, to that church which counted among its apostles Pasqualis Martinez, Saint-Martin and even Mme de Krudemer.

The distinctive characteristic of this school is to avoid publicity and never to grow into what might be referred to as a 'dissident sect'. The count Joseph de Maistre, this radical Catholic, was far more sympathetic than one might think to the society of the Martinistes, thus announcing an impending regeneration of dogma through the lights which shine forth from the sanctuaries of occultism. There exist today fervent priests initiated into antique doctrine and one bishop among others has just died who asked me for Qabalistic information. The disciples of Saint-Martin called themselves the unknown philosophers, and now other disciples of a modern master, fortunate enough to remain anonymous, need take no name at all, for the world does not even suspect their existence. Jesus said that the yeast must be hidden in the bottom of the trough of dough in order that it may work night and day in silence until fermentation of the entire mass has taken place.

An initiate can then with simplicity and sincerity practise the religion into which he was born, for all rites diversely represent one and the same dogma. But no initiate should open the depths of his conscience except to God, nor give account of his most intimate beliefs to anyone. The priest cannot judge that which the Pope himself cannot understand. The exterior signs of the initiate are modest knowledge, philanthropy without show, equality of character and the most inalterable goodness.

Yours in the holy science,
    Eliphas Lévi

APPENDIX
The Doctrine of Eliphas Lévi
by Papus

Introduction to the Study of the Doctrine of Eliphas Lévi
Our aim — Object of this work — Principle influences
which determine the intellectual orientation of Eliphas:
Wronski, the Qabalah

In no way do we conceal from ourselves the heaviness of the task we have undertaken in setting out to make a résumé of the doctrine of Eliphas Lévi. Attempts to gather into several pages ideas he has developed throughout volumes are always at an author's expense; thus we will do our utmost to group together as harmoniously as possible the opinions of Eliphas on the three great subjects whose essence man seeks, namely: himself, the universe and God. We will thus avoid not a few obstacles and we will even follow a teaching of the master, who announces many times that he has been careful with the most secret parts of the doctrine to scatter them here and there throughout several volumes or in the middle of a few chapters otherwise devoted to highly technical matter, so as to sidetrack the curiosity of the hasty or lazy reader.

We will not preface this study with a biography of Eliphas Lévi (Father Constant), as our friend Lucien Mauchel has taken this upon himself, having accumulated for several years now many notes and precious documents.

If we have decided to present the reader with a résumé of the master's ideas at the close of one of his most important posthumous works, it is because we hope to thus repay, however feebly, a debt of profound gratitude. For it is our humble person who was chosen by the occult influences of the invisible as depositary of a large number of the celebrated Qabalist's favourite objects. At present we possess the magic sword of Eliphas Lévi, together with the extract from the will bequeathing this precious object to the friend most faithful in his assistance to the master until the end. We also have the notebook in which are related the experiences of evocation practised in London and Paris, as well as the drawings, finely done, of the apparitions. In addition, the only large photographic portrait made during Eliphas's life hangs in our study. Finally, there are several books which belonged to the celebrated occultist and still more important, precious and unpublished manuscripts, among them *The Book of Splendours*. Our friend Mauchel in his turn has brought together several posthumous works. If we believed in the influence of chance, we would say that all this has been brought about in this way; but we are of the firm conviction that it has all been decided elsewhere.

We must, however, thank the human intermediaries who, without always knowing us well, have done us the great service of bringing to light certain objects and particular memories. First place must be given to the late M.P., testamentary executor, who visited the group of esoteric studies and recounted to Lucien Mauchel the little-known life of the master. Next Eliphas's sword, which was traced by Mlle A. de Wolska, was offered to us by our friend Julien Lejay, who had received it from Me Ve P., its possessor. The baron Spedalieri, an old friend of Eliphas living in Marseille, gave us the master's portrait and a portion of his Qabalistic correspondence. Later the baron offered the full nine volumes of correspondence to Mauchel for publication. Lastly, Me B., through a series of the most mysterious circumstances, put us in possession of most of the posthumous works of the famous Qabalist. We shall see as we continue how the students of Eliphas Lévi,

far more worthy than we of such an honour, might easily
and better have been called to write these pages. However,
if it is not to talent but to devotion that the Invisible
makes its appeal, we do not hesitate to claim one of the
thus merited places.

These are the reasons for our daring, which we felt it
necessary to set down. Now it is time to begin our subject.

First we must establish to the best of our ability the
beginnings of Eliphas's studies. The facts now known
about the master's life show him above all as an artist; a
fervent follower of Tiphereth in all manifestations, it was
only after having grown aware of the cult of beauty that
his generous soul brought him to cultivate goodness and
devote himself to the service of the Divine by taking
orders. Constant's theological studies were later the very
basis of his esoteric deductions and left a profound mark
on his works. But it was to Hoené Wronski that Eliphas
owed the first revelation which propelled him definitely
into the study and practices of the Qabalah. The encounter
of such an enthusiastic and generous artist as Eliphas with
so cold and deductive a thinker as Wronski was to have
singular effects. Thus we will see the profound though
abstract theories of the Pole become under Eliphas's pen
hardy deductions where the most enlightened faith is wed
to the highest principles of general science. Later the
disciple and master were to go their separate ways and
when Eliphas had found his place in the sun, his disciple
Desbarolles generously repaid him in like manner, com-
menting the magic declaration: *the initiate shall kill the
initiator.*

The tiny future quarrels must not allow us, however, to
lose sight of the considerable intellectual influence exercised by Wronski on Eliphas. Especially it is to him that
this latter owes the almost mathematical rigour of his
deductions whose origins are most often purely philosophical. The character of the Qabalist has, however,

remained so dominated by artistic tendencies that occultists from the scientific milieu have some difficulty, at first reading, seizing Eliphas Lévi's true value, whereas the more literary minded are 'sold' from the very beginning.

In order to better characterize the influence of Wronski, let us examine the origin of an affirmation which repeatedly comes back under the master's pen.

Harmony results from the analogy of opposites.

Such is the revelatory law which permitted Eliphas to solve the most obscure problems of the Qabalah.

Where did Eliphas get this law?

We can answer without hesitation: from Wronski.

Wronski's law of creation contains:

1. A ternary-generator, itself generated by the neutral element;

2. A quaternary derived from the combination of the elements of this ternary;

3. A second quaternary, derived from the fusion or reciprocal influence of the primordial elements.

This system, then, reproduces exactly the system of the Sephiroth (the ten Sephir plus the absolute = 11 terms), but by giving the absolute key to Qabalistic revelation, its *physiology,* so to speak.

Now, the ultimate element which synthesizes in itself all oppositions and antagonisms is called by Wronski *coronal parity* (CP) and thus defined: 'CP, ultimate identity in the systematic reunion of two elements derived as distinct from US and UE by means of EN, which they have in common.'

Thus the analogy of opposites results from the fact that these opposites essentially possess a common element. Wronski does more than to simply affirm the reality of the analogy of opposites; he explains it and gives its law.

The study of U.A. (ultimate assistance) would permit us to further develop Wronski's point, but it is sufficient to have shown the origin of Eliphas Lévi's revelation.

But it is not to the Polish mathematician alone that the

master is indebted for the orientation of his work. The Qabalah, necessitating a deep study of the Hebrew language, found in Eliphas Lévi an admirable revelator.

And we say revelator, not popularizer. Occult science cannot be popularized, no more than can the Qabalah; for never will those who 'are not to understand' be able to seize its meaning, in spite of all the clarity in the world.

Thus, the Qabalah and Wronski's law of creation were the principle influences which modified the purely artistic tendencies of Eliphas Lévi.

But we cannot repeat often enough that these tendencies have left such a profound trace on the master's work that the attraction of his books is far greater upon artists and theologians than on the scientists, who instinctively prefer the more learned Fabre d'Olivet or the more mathematical Wronski to the erudite author of *Dogma of High Magic*.

But let us linger no longer over these preliminary considerations, but rather take up the quotes which will demonstrate, better than any commentary, the value of the master's doctrine.

The Doctrine of Eliphas Lévi

In our attempted résumé of Eliphas Lévi's doctrine, we will touch successively upon the following points:

1. 2. 3. Man considered in his general make-up, in the analysis of constituent principles, and in the evolution of these principles.

4. The Universe.

5. God.

6. We will then examine the morality which arises from the thinking of Eliphas Lévi and we will summarize the indications he gives to the occultist as to how to conduct himself in life and in society.

7. Finally, we will conclude with several considerations on the way in which the master used symbolism, a thing he

learned from the higher teachings of the Qabalah.

Once more, we do not claim to give a complete idea of the work of Eliphas Lêvi, but only hope that the variety of subjects treated will allow us to gain an overall picture of a doctrine which has had so profound an influence on our time. Needless to say, we will quote the master himself as often as possible, limiting our role to the choice and placement of the citations.

1.   General Make-Up of Man

'Man is an intelligent corporeal being, made in the image of God and the World, one in essence, triple in substance, both mortal and immortal.

'He is composed of a spiritual soul, a material body and a flexible mediator.'

Such is the superb definition given us by Eliphas Lévi of the human being, thus establishing:

(i)   The rapport between the microcosm (man) and the macrocosm (the Universe), joined by the laws of analogy.

(ii)   The unity of essence and the triplicity of essence, origin both of passion and the power to control it, and source of the many apparent contradictions which human nature presents.

(iii)   The distinction between the mortal and immortal parts of man points to the reason for all contradictions and philosophies, from materialism which takes into account only what is material, to the most exaggerated mysticism which concerns itself only with all that is immortal. This essential distinction is further stressed in another passage where the master says:

'Man is the shadow of God in the body of an animal.'

As regards the comparative role of the sexes, it is defined thus:

'Man is the initiating force which breaks apart, labours and propagates.

'Woman is the forming force which brings together, nourishes and harvests.'

2.   Analysis of Constituent Principles

'Man is composed of a spiritual soul, a material body and a flexible mediator.'

What is the principal point of Eliphas's analysis?

It can easily be guessed. Not the spiritual soul, for in psychology Eliphas has not risen to the heights of Fabre d'Olivet or Wronski. Nor the physical body, for our author, essentially of an artistic nature, would shy away from the technicalities of physiology. No, it is the flexible mediator, the astral body of Paracelsus, well known to ancient philosophers and misunderstood by those of the present day, about which Eliphas has much to say and whose various aspects he brings marvellously to light.

The flexible mediator in man, the astral light in the universe, these are the two revelations given to his century by the author of *Dogma of High Magic*.

Let us leave till later (when discussing evolution) the spiritual soul or *mind*, the highest principle, and take up immediately the study of the flexible mediator. First take this quotation from Postel which unveils one of the most obscure arcana of esoterica: the duality of the second term of any ternary:

> The Trinity created man in its image and likeness. The human body is double and its ternary unity is composed of the union of these two halves; the human soul is also double, it is *animus* and *anima*, spirit and tenderness.
>
> It has two sexes. The paternal sex resides in the head, the maternal, in the heart. The achievement of humanity's redemption must, then, be double: the mind, through its purity, must redeem the aberrations of the heart, and the heart, through its generosity, must redeem the egotistical insensibility of the head.
>
> Postel (quoted by Eliphas)

The Flexible Mediator We give now, without commentary, the following extracts which are mutually explanatory.

That which can be said of the entire soul (infinite perfectibility) can be said of each faculty of the soul.

The intelligence and will of man are instruments of incalculable force and reach.

But intelligence and will have as an auxiliary and instrument another faculty, all too little known and whose omnipotence belongs exclusively to the domain of magic.

I am speaking of imagination, which the Qabalists call the *diaphanus* or translucid.

Imagination is like the eye of the soul. It is here that forms are delineated and preserved. It is here that we glimpse reflections from the invisible world. It is the mirror of visions and the fundamental apparatus of the magical life. It is through the imagination that we heal the sick, influence reason, hold death at bay from the living and resurrect the dead, for it is imagination which exalts the will and gives it a hold over the universal agent.

Imagination determines the shape of the child in its mother's womb, and settles the destinies of men, it gives wings to contagion and guides the weapons of war.

The imagination is the instrument of the World's adaptation.

Imagination applied to reason is genius.

The substance of the flexible mediator is light that is partly mobile, partly fixed.

Mobile part	=	magnetic fluid.
Fixed part	=	fluid or aromal body.

The flexible mediator is formed of astral or terrestrial light and transmits to the human body double magnetism.

Thus, acting on this light by its mobility, it can either dissolve it or cause it to coagulate, project it or attract it. It is the mirror of imagination and dreams. It acts on the nervous system and thereby produces the movements of the body.

This light can spread out indefinitely, communicating its image at considerable distances; it magnetizes bodies subject to the actions of man and can, by shrinking together, attract them to him. It can take on all forms evoked by thought and in the temporary coagulations of its radiating part, it can appear to the eyes and even offer a sort of resistance to contact.

But these manifestations and uses of the flexible mediator being abnormal, the luminous 'precision instrument' cannot produce them without harm to itself, and they cause, without fail, habitual hallucination or madness.

Animal magnetism is the action of one flexible mediator on another for dissolving or coagulating. By augmenting the elasticity of vital light and fixative power, one can send it as far as one wishes and bring it back full of images; but this operation must be aided by the subject's sleep which is produced by further coagulation of the fixed part of the mediator.

There exists a language of sleep which, in the waking state, cannot be comprehended, nor even its words gathered together and set down.

The language of sleep is that of nature, hieroglyphic in its characters and only rhythmic in its sounds.

Our flexible mediator is a magnet which attracts or repels the central light under pressure from the will.

It is a luminous body which reproduces with the greatest facility forms corresponding to ideas.

It is the mirror of the imagination. The mind is nourished by astral light exactly as the organic body is nourished by products of the earth. During sleep it absorbs astral light by immersion, during waking hours, by a series of more or less slow respirations.

Men and things are magnetized with light and, by means of electro-magnetic chains stretched forth by sympathies and affinities, can communicate with one another from one end of the world to the other, caressing or striking, healing or wounding, in a fashion which, though entirely natural, is prodigious and invisible.

Here lies the secret of magic.

Our double magnetism produces in us two sorts of sympathies. We need to absorb and radiate by turns. Our heart likes contrasts, and there are very few examples of women who have loved two men of genius in succession.

The equilibrating factor of each person's flexible mediator is what Paracelsus calls their *ascendant*. And he gives the name of *flagum* to the personal reflection, via astral light, of their habitual ideas.

One arrives at a knowledge of a person's *ascendant* through sensitive divination of the *flagum* and by a perseverant directing of the will: one turns the active side of his own *ascendant* towards another when he wishes to take hold of him and dominate him.

The astral ascendant is a double whirlwind which produces inevitable attractions and determines the form of the astral body.

Evildoers make their ascendant expressive, using it to trouble the ascendant of others.

Paracelsus (quoted by Eliphas Lévi)

The alliance of body and soul is a marriage of light and shadow.

The stars breathe out their luminous souls and attract their radiance one from another.

The soul of the earth, captive of the fatal laws of gravitation, frees itself through specialization, passes through the instincts of animals and arrives at the intelligence of man.

The captive part of this soul is mute; but it keeps nature's secrets in writing. The free part cannot read this fatal writing without instantly losing its liberty. One does not pass from mute, vegetative contemplation to free, living thought except by changing organs and surroundings. From this comes the forgetfulness which accompanies birth and the vague reminiscences of our more morbid intuitions, always analogous to the visions of our ecstasies and dreams.

Paracelsus (quoted by Eliphas)

Ideas produce forms and, in turn, forms reflect and reproduce ideas.

After death, the soul belongs to God and the body to the common mother, which is the earth. Woe to those who disturb this final refuge.

The souls of animals, separated from the body with violence, remain near these animals.

Intoxication is temporary madness and madness is permanent intoxication. Both are caused by a phosphoric overloading of the nerves in the brain and destroy our luminous equilibrium, depriving the soul of its 'precision instrument'.

The fluid, personal soul is then carried off by the fluid material soul of the world (like Moses upon the waters).

The soul of the world is a force which always tends towards equilibrium; the will must triumph over it, or it must triumph over the will.

Existence is substance and life.

Life is manifested through movement and movement is perpetuated by equilibrium.

Thus, equilibrium is the law of immortality. Consciousness is the sense of equilibrium. Equilibrium is justice and justness.

The soul of the earth drags into the vertigo of astral movement all that does not resist it through the balanced forces of reason.

In order to regenerate oneself morally, one must study, understand and put into practice the higher Qabalah.

Body. Regarding *physical body*, we offer the following extracts which develop still further the discussion of the flexible mediator.

'The human unity is made up of right and left. Primitive man was androgynous. All external organs of the human body occur in pairs except the nose, the tongue and the Qabalistic Yod.'

Magnetic influence spreads outwards in two rays from the head, from each hand and foot. The positive ray is equilibrated by the negative ray.

The head corresponds to the feet, each hand to one foot and the other hand, the two feet to the head and one hand.

The human body, as a physical organism, acts in inverse proportion to the alternate preponderance of the two sexes upon the double force of the soul: intellect and sensitivity.

Our body, in human life, is like a useless envelope for the third life, and it is for this reason that we cast it off at the moment of our second birth.

Human life, compared to celestial life, is a veritable embryonic stage. When wicked passions kill us, nature aborts, and we are prematurely reborn for all eternity, which exposes us to that terrible dissolution which St John calls the second death.

Here is the role of the body compared to the soul:

The human soul, served and limited by physical organs, cannot put itself in contact with the things of the visible world except by means of these organs, themselves. The body is an envelope, proportioned to the material surroundings in which the soul must live here below. By limiting the action of the soul, the body concentrates this action and makes it possible. In fact, the soul without the body would be everywhere, but spread so thinly then as to make it impossible for the soul to exist actively anywhere. It would be lost in infinity, absorbed and annihilated, so to speak, in God.

As a matter of curiosity, let us look at the secret of *physical regeneration* transcribed by Eliphas after Cagliostro:

Let us now take up the secret of physical regeneration.

In the month of May, during the full moon,

Alone in the countryside with one loyal assistant,

Fast for a period of forty days, drinking only the May dew, gathered with a pure linen cloth from the spring grasses and eating only tender new stalks and leaves,

With, at the end of the meal, a simple crust of bread, and always beginning with a large glass of dew.

The seventeenth day, perform a light bloodletting.

Each morning take six drops of azote balm, each evening, ten, adding two drops daily until the thirty-second day.

Then repeat the light bloodletting at dawn, followed by

sleep, and remain in bed until the end of the fortieth day.

Upon waking, after the bloodletting, take a grain of universal medicine.

You will then be subject to a fainting spell which should last about three hours, followed by convulsions, perspiration and considerable evacuation; change both clothing and bed linen.

Next drink a light, non-fatty consommé of beef, seasoned with rue, sage, valerian, verbena and melissa.

The following day, take a second grain of universal medicine, that is, of astral mercury mixed with gold sulphur.

The next day, take a lukewarm bath.

The thirty-sixth day, drink a glass of Egyptian wine.

The thirty-seventh day, take a third and final grain of universal medicine.

The hair, teeth and nails will renew themselves, likewise the skin.

The thirty-eighth day, bathe using the afore-mentioned herbs.

Every fifty years, make such a forty-day retreat, considering it a kind of jubilee.

On the thirty-ninth day, swallow ten drops of elixir of Acharat in two spoonfuls of wine.

On the fortieth day, the operation is finished and the old has become young once more.

3. Evolution of Principles

In order to understand what follows, the reader should recall the teachings of the Qabalah concerning the human being and its make-up.

In their general study, the Qabalists do not take into account the physical body of man. They take into consideration only the two polarizations of the intermediary principle between immortal spirit and the body, naming the lesser polarization Nephesh, and the higher, Ruach. Pure spirit takes the name of Neschamah.

Now, the human being during its existence generates the

formative elements of its future existence. Each of us creates his destiny, and the principle of this creation is called by Eliphas the *imago*, the image which will form our future astral body.

The Indians give this principle the name of Karma.

Fabre d'Olivet gives it as the origin of the fate of the human monad, with will enlightened by Providence during incarnation capable of struggling against it.

Thus, in all revelations, we find this same principle clothed in various names.

The reader can now understand the following quotation which explains the evolution of principles.

The soul is clothed light. This light is triple:

Neschamah — pure spirit

Ruach — the soul

Nephesh — the flexible mediator

The clothing of the soul is the outer covering of the image.

The image is double, for it reflects the good and evil angels.

	Neschamah	
Ruach		*Nephesh*
Michael	*Imago*	*Samael*
	Imago	

Nephesh remains immortal, renewing itself by the destruction of forms.

Ruach is in a constant state of progression, through the evolution of ideas.

Neschamah is also progressive, but without forgetfulness and without destruction.

The soul has three dwelling-places:

The home of the living,

The higher eden,

The lower eden.

The *image* is a sphinx, posing the enigma of birth.

The image gives Nephesh its capabilities; but Ruach can replace it with the image itself, conquered, as it were, through the inspiration of Neschamah.

The body is the mould of Nephesh, Nephesh is the mould of Ruach, Ruach is the mould of the outer covering of Neschamah.

Light is personified by taking on this outer covering and personality is stable only when the covering is perfect.

This perfection on earth is relative to the universal soul of the world.

There are three atmospheres in which souls can dwell.

The third leaves off where the planetary attraction of other worlds begins.

Souls which have reached perfection on earth depart for another station.

Having visited the planets, they go to the sun.

From there they rise to other universes and begin again their evolution from world to world and from sun to sun.

Within the suns they remember all; upon the planets they forget.

The solar lives are the days of eternal existence, and the planetary lives are the nights, with their dreams.

Angels are luminous emanations, personified, not by trial and the taking on of outer form, but by reflection and divine influence.

Angels aspire to become men; a perfect man, a man-God is above all angels.

Planetary lives are composed of ten dreams, each lasting 100 years. Each solar life has a duration of 1,000 years. Thus it is said that before God, a thousand years are as a single day.

Every week, that is, every 14,000 years, the soul is retempered, reposing in the jubilate sleep of forgetfulness.

On waking, it has forgotten evil and remembers only the good; it is a new birth, a new week begins.

Matter *cloaks* the spirit, and AFTERWARDS, spirit must gradually rid itself of this covering, in the fertility of divine warmth.

4. The Universe

As we have said, Eliphas sought above all to elucidate the role of the flexible mediator in man and of astral light in nature.

Thus, without lingering overlong upon the three divisions of the macrocosm, the great Qabalist returns again and again to his favourite subject: astral light or the beings which inhabit it, elementary spirits or others.

And so we are going to reproduce a series of quotations, most interesting to compare, and which have a bearing on one of these two points, an understanding of which is so useful to any serious occultist.

Astral Light

All these wonders occur by means of a single agent which the Hebrews, like the Chevalier de Reichenbach, called OD, and which we shall refer to as astral light, following in this the school of Martinez Pasqualis. (M. de Mirville calls it the Devil, and the ancient alchemists named it Azoth.) It is the vital element, manifesting itself in the phenomena of warmth, light, electricity and magnetism, and flowing through all terrestrial globes and all living beings. Within this very agent are manifested the proofs of Qabalistic doctrine regarding equilibrium and the movement of double polarity, one pole attracting while the other repels, one producing heat and the other cold, one giving a blue-greenish light and the other a yellow-reddish glow.

By its different modes of influence, this agent attracts some of us to others, keeps us away from still others, submits one person to another's will by drawing him into the former's circle of attraction, re-establishes or disturbs equilibrium by its transmutations and alternating currents, receives and transmits the imprint of imagination's force (which in man is the image and likeness of the creative word), and in addition produces presentiments and determines the nature of dreams. The science of miracles, then, is the knowledge of this wondrous force, and the art of performing miracles is simply the art of *illuminating* or influencing other beings in accordance with the invariable laws of magnetism or astral light.

We prefer the word *light* to that of *magnetism*, for it is more traditional to occultism and expresses the nature of the secret agent in a more complete and perfect way. Without doubt, this is the potable fluid gold of the alchemists; the word gold (= *or*) comes from the Hebrew *aour* which signifies 'light'. What do you desire? This is an age-old question asked of all initiates. And this is the response: To see the light. The name of *illuminati* has been commonly given to all adepts of occultism, though generally misinterpreted to signify men who believe themselves enlightened by a miraculous light. *Illuminati* simply means possessors of light, whether it be due to a scientific study of the great magical agent or to a rational, ontological notion of the absolute.

The universal agent is vital force subordinate to intelligence. Left to itself, it rapidly devours, like Moloch, everything to which it gives birth, changing the abundance of life to a vast destruction. Then it is the infernal Serpent of the ancient myths, the Typhon of the Egyptians, the Moloch of the Phoenicians; but if wisdom, mother of Elohim, places her foot on its head, she quenches all the flames he spews forth and pours out upon the earth abundantly a life-giving light. Thus it is said in the Sohar that at the beginning of our earthly period, when the elements quarrelled for control of the world's surface, fire, like an immense serpent, enveloped everything in its coils and was on the point of consuming all beings when divine mercy, raising around itself the waves of the sea like a cloak of clouds, placed a foot on the serpent's head and sent him back into the abyss. Who cannot see in this allegory the first premise and most reasonable explanation for one of the images so cherished by Catholic symbolism: the triumph *of the mother* of God?

The Creation of Beings by Means of Light

Light is the efficient agent of form and life, for it is both movement and heat. When it succeeds in fixing itself, polarized round a centre, it produces a living being; then in order to perfect and preserve it, it attracts whatever plastic or flexible substance is necessary. This substance, in the final analysis formed of earth and water, was rightly called by the Bible the 'clay of the earth'.

But light is not spirit as the Indian hierophants believe; it is only an instrument of spirit. It is not the body of the *photoplases* as the theurgists of the Alexandrian School gave to believe; it is the primary physical manifestation of divine breath. God creates it eternally, and man, in the image of God, modifies it and seems to multiply it.

One should avoid the fatal forces; it is pretentious to affront them or try to destroy them.

If a cannon-ball hurtles towards you over the ground, don't try to stop it, move out of its path.

These fatal forces are the magnetic powers of the earth, figured in the two serpents of the caduceus;

And by astral light, which the Hebrews call *od* when it is active, *ob* when it is passive and *aour* when it is equilibrated;

And by the two serpents of Hermes, one blue and the other red, entwined around a silver sceptre with a golden head.

These forces are the perpetual movement of the clock of centuries; when one serpent contracts, the other loosens its hold.

These forces break those who do not know how to direct them. They are the two snakes at the cradle of Hercules.

The child takes one in each hand, the red in the right and the blue in the left.

Thus they die and their power passes into the arms of Hercules.

Let all adepts of magnetism ponder, study and understand this mystery.

For to become master of these two serpents, one must unite them on the caduceus of Hermes or separate them with the strength of Hercules.

In the soul of the world there is a current of love and a current of wrath (ouroboros – the belt of Isis).

Movement and life consist of the profound tension of these two forces.

Matter is the external form of spirit. Intelligence acts upon it and it reacts in turn upon intelligence. Harmony results from the analogy of these two contrary forces.

By gaining control of thought, which produces various forms, one becomes master of these forms, capable of using them for one's own ends. Astral light is saturated with souls which it gives off continually in the unceasing generation of beings. Souls have imperfect wills which can be dominated and used by wills of greater strength; thus they form great invisible chains and can occasion or determine vast elemental upheavals.

Of demons
Certain critics, poorly informed as to the traditional doctrines of occultism, have tried to claim that occultists were not in agreement concerning the existence of mortal demons and elementaries.

We have personally demonstrated the inanity of this claim, aided by numerous citations drawn from authors from widely diverse epochs. Here are two extracts from the writings of Eliphas which throw light on the question. It will be seen that he says expressly that 'elemental spirits' are *mortal*.

This is, then, the division we ourselves have proposed, that of mortal spirits or *elementals* and immortal (as regards their essence) spirits or elementaries.

Fluid Phantoms and Their Mysteries

The ancients gave them different names, such as *larvae, lemures*. They were reputed to thrive on the vapours exuded from spilt blood, but fled from any naked sword.

Theurgy called them forth in evocation, and the Qabalah knew them under the name of elemental spirits.

They were not spirits, however, for they were mortal.

They were fluid coagulations which could be destroyed.

They were a kind of animate mirage, imperfect emanations of human life. The traditions of black magic say that they were born during the celibacy of Adam. Paracelsus claims that the vapours from the blood of menstruating women people the air with phantoms; and such ideas are so old that we find their trace in Hesiod, who expressly forbids leaving soiled linen of any nature to dry before a fire.

Persons obsessed with phantoms are ordinarily overstrung because of a too rigorous self-imposed celibacy or weakened by the excesses of debauchery.

Fluid phantoms are the abortions of vital light; they are flexible mediators without body and without spirit, born from excesses of the mind and dissipations of the body.

These wandering mediators can be attracted by certain sick people who are inevitably sympathetic to them, lending them, at their own expense, a more or less durable artificial existence. At such times these phantoms play the role of instruments supplementary to the instinctive wills of these sick ones, never however working to cure them but instead weakening them and causing their minds to stray and hallucinate all the more.

Elemental Demons

Created spirits, drawn to emancipation through trials, are

from their birth placed at a mid-point among four forces, two positive and two negative, capable of affirming or denying goodness, of choosing life or death.

To find the finite point, that is, the moral centre of the cross, is the first problem which they are given to solve; their first victory must be that of winning their own freedom.

They begin, then, by being attracted some to the north, some to the south, some to the right, others to the left, and as long as they are not free, they are denied the use of reason and cannot assume an incarnation other than in animal forms. These unemancipated spirits, slaves of the four elements, are what the Qabalists call elemental demons, and they inhabit the elements which correspond to their state of servitude. Sylphs, undines, salamanders and gnomes actually exist, some roaming abroad in search of incarnation, the others incarnate and wandering about on the earth; these latter are wicked and imperfect men.

5. God

Generally speaking, no question is quite so troubling to philosophers than that of Divinity and its attributes. But the Qabalist, armed with far more precise keys than reason normally furnishes, need not be afraid to take up this awesome problem which touches the great incommunicable arcanum so closely.

Following the examples of his masters, Wronski and the Qabalah, Eliphas chooses not to reveal the great Arcanum. In his wonderful *Credo*, he begins thus:

'I believe in the *Unknown* which God PERSONIFIES, whose existence is proved by Being itself and by immensity, the SUPERHUMAN ideal of philosophy; perfect intelligence and supreme goodness.'

Only ecstasy and illumination permit the attainment of this *superhuman* ideal.

The following quotations from the master develop perfectly his ideas. Let us not forget, however, that a completely defined God is a finite God.

The Qabalists consider God to be intelligent, loving, living infinity. For them he is not the totality of beings, nor the abstraction of Being, nor any philosophically definable being whatsoever. He is in everything, yet both distinct from and greater than everything. His name is unutterable, although this name is only an expression of the human ideal of his divinity. All that God is unto himself has not been given to man to understand.

GOD is faith's absolute; reason's absolute is BEING.

Being exists of itself, because it is; it is its own reason for being.

This incontestable philosophical reality, which has been called the idea of God, has been given a name by the Qabalists; it is a name which contains all others. All numbers are derived from the digits of this name; the hieroglyphs of its letters express all the laws of nature.

As we have said, they appreciate the worth of divine realities made manifest in their mirage or shadow within the human mind, but they believe this shadow or mirage to exist in exact reverse of the realities it results from. It is therefore the task of science to set the matter right, arriving at the harmony which comes from the analogy of opposites.

The perception of common things through antithesis is one of the greatest secrets of the Qabalah.

I — X (series of Latin quotes)

Pythagorus thus defined God: an absolute and living truth, clothed in light.

He said the Word was number manifested in form.

God is the soul of light.

For us, universal, infinite light is the body of God.

The peoples of the world make idols and break them, hell

is inhabited by gods who shall remain fallen until the word of the great initiator is heard: God is spirit and we must worship him in spirit and in truth!

On Religion

Cults come and go, but religion is always the same; dogmas prey upon each other like wild beasts; yet the dogmatic world is no more the domain of error than the earthly world is the empire of death. Real life feeds upon apparent death, and sooner or later all religious controversies must come to an end in a vast catholicity. Then humanity will know why it has suffered, and eternal life, by disarming the angel of death, will reveal to all nations the mystery of pain.

Lastly, let us emphasize this remark, which we offer gladly for the admiration of 'those who know':

God is at work in heaven through his angels and on the earth, through man.

6. Realization of the Doctrine:
Moral Conclusions – The Magic Axioms

Having taken a rapid overall look at the doctrine of Eliphas, a doctrine derived almost exclusively from the Qabalah (but adapted to our times with such art!), we are now going to attempt to examine how the master sees the realization of this doctrine, how man, controlling his own passions, can aspire to a veritable magical way of life.

The master sets down three principal rules: to know how to *suffer, abstain* and *die*. In his own words: 'Learning to suffer, learning to die, these are the practical exercises of eternity, the immortal novitiate.'

Thus the student of occult science should first of all dominate the prejudices which surround such study, understanding that Magic and Esoterica are only *occult* for the ambitious and the ignorant.

The Occult Sciences

There are men who are vexed and tired by the light and who, turning their backs on the sun, look only at their own shadows.

If they think themselves Christian, then they worship the Devil, giving him the attributes of God.

If they call themselves philosophers, they worship nothingness and anarchy, wishing to substitute these for the eternal being and immutable order which presides over the hierarchy of beings.

Audacious affirmation and absurd negation also have their fanatics; these are the night creatures of intelligence.

They see nothing, except by the night of their passion; when it is day, they grow blind.

Such men will never understand anything of occult philosophy

And it is for them alone that it remains occult.

As occult as the sun for the creatures of night;

As occult as common sense for the fanatics of the world;

As occult as reason for the truly mad.

For occultism is the philosophy of light, the philosophy of common sense, the philosophy of exactitude, as precise as numbers, as rigorous as the proportions of geometry, as evident as being, and as infallible as the mathematics of eternity.

He is blind who does not see it; but he is all the more blind who claims to see it by night!

The man who is so bold as to look upon the sun without shade becomes blind; then the sun, for him, is a blackness.

Never will the stupid and vulgar comprehend the high wisdom of the Magi! Orpheus sings and common monkeys make faces. What else can we expect? They believe the poet is singing praises to their own commonplace tails! The honours one asks of the masses are a bitter ambrosia, for they contain much gall and little honey; the immortal palm is slow to mature and lends shade to scarcely nothing but the grave. True great men are not anxious for the recognition of their glory; they know that if lightning spares the laurel it is only by a sort of complicity among catastrophes (Fable IV); a laurel crown is all too often a crown of confusion. The sap of the laurel contains the most subtle of all poisons.

Yes, one must be daring to seriously involve oneself with this occult philosophy which has been treated with such scorn by those who deny its truth and with such hate by those who attribute its existence to the Devil; one must be daring to control the vital light which prolongs the effect of our organs far beyond even their visible limits and which permeates with our own life the objects we choose to employ. One must be daring to gain supremacy over the phantoms of imagination and the worries of the mind; one must be daring to think differently from the vulgar, opposing the immutable reason of the wise to the ever-changing incoherence of the common crowd. God has placed peace and happiness at our disposition; but one must reach out and touch the fruits of the tree of life, forbidden by so much prejudice, so many idle dreams. And one must dare to take these fruits, steal them, as it were; for as soon as we have picked them, nature gives them to us freely. Let us not forget that heaven admits the force of violence and begs to be taken by storm.

If hell were to be the birthright of courageous intelligence, struggling in the name of reason, and if heaven were reserved for fearful stupidity, ever ready to blindly obey, then men of honour and heart should all enter hell, and hell would become a new heaven.
Love, this is Magic's great secret; but one must distinguish between the love that gives immortality and the love that kills.

'As long as love is only desire and pleasure, it is mortal. To become eternal it must become a sacrifice, for it is only then that love becomes a force and a virtue. It is the struggle of Eros and Anteros which creates the equilibrium of the world.'

This is why hate produces tears and remorse.

Our hate makes our enemies strong. The only way to render them powerless to harm us is to love them.

The love of our enemies is the strongest of all loves, for it is the most generous and as a consequence, the most tranquil.

He who hates, hates himself; he who strikes out, strikes out at himself; he who curses, curses himself; he who breaks is broken.

The soul of the wicked is eternally devoured by the monsters it gives birth to.

A feeling of hate or envy is a viper which one warms and nourishes within one's heart.

Evil feelings often take on the hideous shapes which correspond to them, and so pursue the wicked in their hallucinations and dreams.

Incurable madness is always a consequence of any mortal sin against justice.

Reason dies from a mortal sin, as the body from a mortal blow.

In malevolam animam non habitabit sapientia, said Solomon. Which means: reason and hate can never dwell side by side.

Whatever your brother may have done to you, if you hate him you are wrong to do so and it is you who are guilty towards him.

Pride

But the occultist must take care. The force he gains may make him forget his veritable mission as an apostle of social evolution, and pride, that supreme temptation, may take possession of his being.

The further man has risen, the greater the disorder which reigns when he abandons himself to the fatality of his instincts. The intoxication of pride is far more unreasonable than that of wine, and the most learned man, should he go astray, is open to lessons in sense and wisdom from even the most worthless being.

Social Ideas

It is from such thinking that derive the social ideas expressed – but with what reserve! – by the great Qabalist and tending towards the establishment of an empire of the wise, governed by a great pope (spiritually) assisted by a great king (temporally).

> Who will put an end to our misery?
> A great pope aided by a great king,
> Destroying all foreign weapons
> To unite progress and faith.

Man has no other master when he is master of himself, and if there existed a nation made up entirely of the wise, it would be a nation of kings. Then only a republic would be possible, for such a people would have no need to be governed. But when I see a populace dulled by drunkenness, an insouciant bourgeoisie caring only for profit and gain, a Press impassioned by self-interest and more often than not calculatedly false, an aristocracy which slips foolishly into decadence, then I wonder what kind of republic it can be they live in, and I suppose that when they cry out for greater liberty it is only that they may behave even more wickedly than they do. It's a fine thing, this declaration of the rights of man; but one should begin by creating men before their rights are given them. I doubt that you could call men the vile multitude that dragged Bailly to the scaffold, whipping him with a mud-spattered flag. If you asked me to what such men have a right, I would answer: to the gunfire of the thirteen Vendémiaire, and such did they in fact encounter ... inevitably.

Republics are not governments, but social crises. When

power, like the stone of Sysiphus, falls from the arms which seek to push it too far, it *rolls down again* to the bottom of the mountain: this is what is called a *revolution*. A thousand arms take hold of this stone to move it, this is the republic; a stronger one comes and picks it up, this is the empire; and he who succeeds in bringing it securely to rest at the mountain's summit establishes a kingdom.

The Magic Realizations of Eliphas

The ignorant fools who study occult science and claim (modestly) to 'profess to them' are generally prey to elementary spirits from the astral plane. They imagine that Magic consists of moving tables and visiting a mistress in an 'astral body'. The phenomena of magical realization which are produced by he who is deeply ingrained with *traditional initiation*, who has found his place in the invisible, are less showy and all the more serious. Any intense desire becomes certain reality within a few days for the true occultist. We could at this very moment cite proofs (infinitely strange to the profane) of the discovery of objects or valuable books following from orderly ideas pursued magically, that is, with will and persevering faith. What we have said in the introduction to this study should suffice to clarify what we only touch on here, and let us now bring to the reader's attention the two following extracts, drawn from Fables and Symbols:

M. Louis Lucas, learned inventor of the biometer, has already demonstrated, following the ideas of the ancients, that all substance is one, owing its particular forms only to the diversity of its modes of molecular polarization and the various *angulations* of its magnetic influence. The consequence of this discovery is that all beings are individual magnets whose life is the work of attraction-repulsion. This daring chemist does not shy away from the hermetic problem and the discovery of potassium seems to have put him on the track of forming the mercury of the sage. He has found that the ancients were acquainted with oxygen under various names ... We can go still further and affirm that they were likewise no strangers to the mysteries of electro-magnetism. We have rediscovered the *pantarbus* of Apollonius, this metal which is also a stone, this stone which is a fruit, this fruit that both radiates and is without light. We know why the mother of the gods was worshipped in the form of a black stone called Elagabale, and how water and fire are drawn from the earth by means of fire issued from water and earth. What we say is perhaps too much for the profane; it is enough for the adepts. And we are reassured by the fact that there is no danger in telling all to the profane, for they will not understand, and if they did, would not believe.

Poverty is almost always more useful to man than wealth, and yet how many times have we experienced that omnipotence of the universal magnet which satisfies all needs and fulfils all desires of the adept, providing they are not unsound? We have even reached the point, as in the children's story *The Three Wishes*, of dreading the casual expression of some vague thoughtless desire. Science brings us its lost or forgotten books; the earth renders up its old talismans. Wealth, its hands full of gold, passes before us and smilingly says: Take all you need. Our dwelling-place is a palace, our life a long feast, yet we still encounter naïve men who toss their heads and say: Prove the power of your doctrine with miracles!

We gave them our answer last year by publishing the *Sorcerer of Meudon*, a study on Rabelais, which is also in some small way our biography: in it we made clear to true Pantagruelists what the wise author of gargantuan madness meant by the oracle of the divine bottle: DRINK!

The Axioms

As an end to this section, let us give the twenty-two fundamental axioms which should guide all occultists aspiring to great magical realizations:

1. Nothing resists man's will when he knows the truth and desires goodness.

2. To wish for evil is to wish for death. A perverse will is the beginning of suicide.

3. To wish for goodness with violence is to wish for evil; for violence produces disorder and disorder produces evil.

4. One can and should accept evil as a means to good, but never wish for it nor do it, for in so doing one tears down with one hand what one builds up with the other. Faith, however good, never justifies evil means; it corrects them when one finds oneself their victim and condemns them when one takes them as one's own.

5. To obtain the right to lasting possession, one must want and wait patiently and for a long time.

6. To spend one's life wanting that which cannot be eternally possessed is to abdicate from life and accept the eternity of death.

7. The more obstacles surmounted by the will, the stronger it grows. It is for this that Christ praised poverty and pain.

8. When the will is dedicated to that which is absurd, it is censured by eternal reason.

9. The will of the just man is the will of God himself and the law of nature.

10. It is through the will that intelligence sees. If the will is healthy, sight is true. God said, 'Let there be Light!' and there is Light. The will says, 'Let the world be as I wish to see it,' and the intelligence sees what the will desires. This is the significance of *So be it*, which accompanies all acts of faith.

11. When one creates phantoms, one brings vampires into the world; and these children of voluntary nightmare must be nourished with one's own blood, one's own life, one's own intelligence and reason; but they are never satisfied.

12. To create is to affirm and desire that which ought to be; to affirm and desire that which ought not to be is to destroy.

13. Light is an electric fire placed in the service of will by nature; it lights the way for those who know its true use; it burns those who would use it wrongly.

14. The empire of the world is the empire of light.

15. Great intelligences accompanied by poorly equilibrated wills are like comets, aborted suns.

16. To do nothing is as disastrous as to do evil, but it is even more cowardly. The most impardonable of mortal sins is inactivity.

17. Suffering is work. To suffer a great pain is to progress most certainly. Those who suffer much live more fully than those who do not suffer at all.

18. Voluntary death through devotion is not suicide; it is the apotheosis of will.

19. Fear is only a laziness of the will; and it is for this reason that the opinion of others is a curse for cowards.

20. Get to the point of not fearing the lion and the lion will fear you. Say to pain and suffering: I want you to be a pleasure, and they will become a pleasure, and even more than this, a blessed thing.

21. A chain of iron is more easily broken than a chain of flowers.

22. Before you declare a man to be happy or unhappy you must know what his control of will has made of him; Tiberius died a daily death on Capri and Jesus gave continual proof of his immortality and divinity even on Calvary.

7. Adaptation of the Doctrine — Symbolism

Nowhere better than in his written works does Eliphas reveal himself to be an accomplished occultist-magician. We would have to offer an entire volume of quotations if we were to adequately demonstrate the boldness of his adaptations, the beauty and grandeur of his poetic images, the knowledgeable precision of his theoretical teachings relative to symbolism and the Qabalah.

Let us begin with the fundamentals of the esoteric

tradition and several citations concerning the Qabalah.

This tradition posits:

1. The existence of a primitive, universal revelation explaining all the secrets of nature and bringing them into harmony with the mysteries of grace; and reconciling reason and faith, for both are the daughters of God and combine to illuminate the intelligence with their double light.

2. The necessity which has always existed of keeping this revelation from the multitudes for fear that they might misuse it, misinterpret it and bring the forces of reason, or even of faith itself, to play against the force of faith.

3. The existence of a secret tradition reserving the knowledge of these mysteries for the sovereign pontiffs and temporal masters of this world.

4. The perpetuity of certain signs or pentacles expressing these mysteries in a hieroglyphic manner and known only to the adepts of the science.

Just as there are three divine notions and three knowable reigns, there is a triple Word; for the hierarchical order always manifests itself in threes. There is the simple word, the hieroglyphic word and the symbolic word. In other words, there is the word which expresses, the word which hides and the word which signifies; all hieratic understanding lies in the science of these three degrees.

The Qabalistic Keys

Authority, that great thing so misunderstood in our time, is based on wisdom and intelligence, like the Kether of the Hebrews with Chokmah and Binah (see our *Dogma and Ritual of High Magic*). Authority sanctions honour which rests on devotion and justice, like Tiphereth on Gedulah and Geburah. Man bases himself on social truth, which is the alliance of order and progress, of law and liberty, of power and duty, and this truth constitutes the moral life of humanity.

Thus:

Authority	1	Honour	6
Wisdom	2	Progress	7
Intelligence	3	Order	8
Devotion	4	Social truth	9
Justice	5	Humanity	10

This is the explanation and philosophical application of the sacred numbers of the Qabalah, whose hieratic and mysterious meanings we have given in our preceding works.

To pronounce the great words of the Qabalah in accordance with Science, they must be pronounced with entire understanding, with a will which nothing hinders, with an active drive which nothing can forestall. In magic, to have spoken is to have done; the word begins with letters and concludes in action.

One does not really desire something unless one wants it with all one's heart, to the point of sacrificing one's most cherished affections, of risking one's health, one's fortune and one's life.

Let us especially bring the reader's attention to this definition of occultism:

Unique dogma, a symbolism at once philosophical and poetical, buried in the ruins of ancient civilizations and reborn in new societies; occultism is beautiful; it is immortal in its profound reason-for-being, it represents nature and its laws, the human spirit and its aspirations, the unknown with its uncertainties overcome by a legitimate hypothesis; but the sweet mysticism of Christianity with its dreams of heaven, its whimperings for an ideal of tenderness and infinite purity, has very nearly obliterated the colossal science of Eleusis and Thebes. Antigone, the ancient virgin, was not a mother, like Mary. We have fewer tears for the innocent daughter of Oedipus, the sacrilege, than for the virgin mother of the Redeemer. The phoenix, always reborn, offers something terrible and exhausting as an image, recalling the vulture of Prometheus; but the Christian dove, carrying in its beak the olive branch, speaks only of love, of mercy and peace.

It is not our wish to resurrect the phoenix in order to oppose it to the Christian dove, but rather that the phoenix render homage to the dove and that the dove console the phoenix in its solitude. We desire that the dogmas of science and of faith be united in a single radiant circle, as the Rosicrucians, our masters, united the graceful image of the rose with the harsh symbol of the cross.

Symbolism and its Applications

It is from the Kabbala that Eliphas draws his conception of symbolism as we shall see it defined and applied in what follows:

Symbolism

Symbolism is a science like algebra, and even analogous to algebra, for, with conventional signs, it abstractly represents ideas as exact as numbers, often making use of numbers themselves for this representation.

The Polish Qabalist Wronski, representing the known and the unknown by Fx, thus uses algebraic characters to pose the universal problem of occult philosophy:

$$Fx = A \_ = A, , + A_2, 2 + A_3 3.$$

Which means: being is proportionate to being, or infinity equals the sum of all possible qualities; or yet again, the absolute properties of being are proportionate to the absolute needs of all beings; from which this axiom can be deduced: the necessity of infinite being supposes the indefinable progress of beings.

Applications of Qabalistic Symbolism

It is said that the life of the rose is short, and yet the rose is always living. Is there ever a springtime without roses?

The rose, as a type, is immortal in light: light ceaselessly captures the reality of roses on vegetable leaves composed of earth and water.

Trials perish and return; but the rose of light does not die.

It is thus with all beautiful things; beauty is eternal, but the clouds it colours with its light are capable of dissolution.

The method of Qabalistic rabbis was to exaggerate symbols in order to explain them; thus they covered the veil with a new one in order to force intelligence to uncover the spirit within the obvious absurdity of the letter.

These same rabbis say also that the cries of women in childbirth are gathered up by the angel of mercy and closed in a golden box, and that on the last day, when Satan will prosecute the human race before the tribunal of God and when men will have of themselves no answer, the angel will open the box; out of it will come a voice more powerful than all the noise of hell, and all the children of Adam will be saved by this sublime defence formed out of a single cry: the liberating cry of all mothers!

Saint Michael and Satan are as a résumé of all symbolism, like Mithra and the black bull, like Hercules and the hydra, like Bellerophon and the chimera, like Apollo and the serpent risen out of the mire of the flood.

Eternal symbolism, like that of light and shadow, thought and form, fable and truth.

Well equilibrated men are centres of movement: they are suns which necessarily draw worlds into their circle of attraction, thus creating universes. This is accomplished of itself, without need for thought, and this is why Christ said: first seek the kingdom of God (truth) and its justice and all the rest shall follow of its own accord. Happy are they who can understand this great word!

Balanced forces are essentially creative. The Elohim made the world and the Elohim are the equilibrating forces of nature. It is for this that, following the Oriental fable, Solomon gave the Queen of Sheba a son, having initiated

her into veritable wisdom. (Fable III) From the line of
Solomon and the Queen of Sheba were born the three
magi-kings who came to visit the Saviour in Bethlehem,
thereby uniting in a simple temple, albeit only a poor
stable, under the rays of a single star, the pentagram of
occult understanding (see our *Dogma and Ritual of High
Magic*) and all symbolisms of the world.

The Great Symbols, Synthesis of the Doctrine
The Sphinx — *The Science of Fate*

The sphinx was seated on his solitary rock,
Proposing an enigma to all prostrate men.
And if the future king succumbed to the mystery,
The monster said: Die, you have not guessed the answer!

Yes, for man here below, life is a problem
Solved by work under the scythe of Death.
The source of the future lies within ourselves
And the sceptre of the world belongs to the strongest.

To suffer is to work, to accomplish one's task!
Woe to the lazy one who sleeps on the road!
Pain, like a dog, nips at the coward's heels,
The coward, who by losing a single day, overburdens the
    next.

To hesitate is to die; error is a crime
Foreseen by nature and paid for in advance.
The angel, not wholly freed, falls again into the abyss,
Kingdom and despair of Satan cast down!

God has never pitied clamourings nor tears,
For our consolation, all the future is there.
We are the ones to forge weapons of misfortune,
God has given us charge of our own chastisement.

To dominate death, one must conquer life,

One must learn how to die, to live again immortal;
Servile nature must be trampled underfoot,
To change man to a sage and the tomb to an altar!

The final word of the sphinx is Alcidius's pyre,
Oedipus's lightning bolt and the Saviour's cross.
To block the efforts of the deicidal serpent,
Pain must be consecrated to holy love!

The human face of the sphinx speaks of understanding,
Its breasts of love, its claws of combat;
Its wings are faith, dream and hope,
And its flanks represent work here below!

If you know how to work, to believe, to love, to
  withstand,
If you are not a prisoner of lowly needs,
If your heart knows how to want and your mind to
  understand,
King of Thebes! Welcome! Here is your crown!

The Philosophical Credo

I believe in the unknown, personified by God:
Proven by being, itself, and by immensity,
Superhuman ideal of philosophy,
Perfect intelligence and supreme goodness.

I believe in the infinite which the finite proclaims;
I believe in reason which never grows weak;
I believe in hope and I have glimpsed the soul,
By feeling that love is scornful of death!

I believe for us that the ideal is realized
In men of love, of spirit, of goodness.
Just people of all times, you are my Church,
And my dogma has universality as its law.

I believe that pain is the effort of being born,
That evil is the shadow or error of good,
That man must win his own being through work,
That goodness is love and that Satan is nothing.

I believe that a single hope lies beneath all symbols,
That solidarity is the law of the world;
I overturn the altars of all idols
By pronouncing two words: justice and truth.

I believe that duty is measured by right,
That the stronger owes more and the weaker, less:
That to fear the true God is to insult him,
That we must unite our efforts in attending him.

I believe that nature is an innocent force
Which our error cannot, with impunity, misuse;
Evil makes the mind watchful and active,
But it is a remedy, not a punishment.

I believe that upon rending the veils of death
We will all return to the paternal home:
Ignorance and error are the shadows of the stars
Whose radiant goodness is the eternal centre!

The Temple of the Future

Divine masters of the empire of dreams,
Great men of hope and kings of memory,
You who change swords to fruitful ploughshares,
I salute you, priests of the future!

Come and bless the immense chain of hearts,
Open space to immortal desires;
The cycle begins again under a new sky,
Humanity rebuilds its altars!

Living numbers of the mute Pythagorus,
Tell us of life in letters of gold.
Draw dawn's rainbow seven times,
It still gives life to Plato's word!
Eternal Christ, monarch of light,
Triumph yet again over your cruel executioners:
Come and transfigure the earth through mind.
Humanity rebuilds its altars!

All the universe is only a sublime temple
With a single king, a single sun, a single God.
Error, night, ignorance and crime
Are dead wood devoured by fire.
Here Zoroaster's faith shines forth;
Hell quenches its eternal pyres,
Psyche smiles and love gives her a crown:
Humanity rebuilds its altars!

Queen of heaven, austere Parthenos,
Come and lay low Typhon's ugliness,
And in the form of Venus Urania
Become the ideal of holy modesty!
Tender Mary with the pure and simple brow,
Explain at last your maternal dogmas;
Be the celestial virgin of our seasons;
Humanity rebuilds its altars!

You whose hell gave out life,
Noble Osiris of Egypt's dreams,
Come to tell the ravished earth again
That Isis has found you, covered with blood.
Beautiful Adonis, make us see that Aphrodite
Can still render her lovers immortal.
Let the Saviour resurrect Christians!
Humanity rebuilds its altars!

Men made God, sing the praise of God made man!

Give a sceptre to the old father Uranus
And let the key of Rome's Saint Peter
Lock the temple of Janus forever.

The world takes communion with sacred bread,
Wine flows and blesses fraternal banquets;
The final orthodoxy is harmony:
Humanity rebuilds its altars!

Form

Thus far we have analysed in particular the content of Eliphas Lévi's doctrine. As regards the form in which the master's ideas are exposed, we must leave the task to those more competent than ourselves, and it is our pleasure to conclude this study of the great Qabalist's doctrine with the following critique, written by one of the master's finest students, and if I may say so, his veritable continuator: I speak of Stanislas de Guaita, the savant and erudite author of *On the Threshold of Mystery* and *Serpent of Genesis*, the president of the Supreme Council of the Rosicrucian Qabalistic Order.

Eliphas Lévi Regarded by Stanislas de Guaita

I see them all, all these philosophers and erudite, knowledgeable men, most of them responsible for a dazzling shower of discoveries, I see them grouped around the great harvester of light; I see them escorting an adept who stands head and shoulders above them and seems, among all these grand barons of renewed esoteric study, to be the *Prince Charming*, spouse by right of conquest of that *Sleeping Beauty* whose name is traditional truth!

Truly, in our own time a genius has manifested himself in order to rebuild the temple, more sumptuous and colossal than ever before, of Solomon the king. With far-reaching thought and spirit of synthesis, with a luminous, rich style, with imperturbable logic and assured science, Eliphas Lévi is an occultist who lacks nothing. The concentric circles of his work embrace *all Science*, and each of his books, displaying a precise meaning, has its absolute reason-for-being. His *Dogma* teaches; his *Ritual* prescribes; his *History* adapts; his *Keys to the Great Mysteries* explains; his *Fables and Symbols* reveals*; his *Sorcerer of Meudon* preaches by example; and finally, his *Science of Spirits* offers a solution to the highest metaphysical problems.

Thus, under Eliphas's pen magic is exposed in all its facets; his total output constitutes the most cohesive, absolute and unchallengeable synthesis an occultist could dream of. And this magnificent thinker has taken it upon himself to become a great artist in addition! His warm, wide, eloquent style, at times scrupulously precise, at times free and bold, encases a thought that is wider and bolder still. Thought-provoking words abound, dizzying 'suggestions' which belie mere verbal expression, subtle nuances defy abstract language, the rigid exactitude of a new metaphor stabilizes the unstable, makes the uncertain precise, defines the immense and numbers the innumerable.

But in his thorough journey through the three worlds – metaphysical, moral and natural – Eliphas Lévi scarcely stops a moment anywhere; the great centralizing current takes him in its wake and many questions he broaches call for further development. Examples would be the Asiatic origins of occultism and social theory, subjects which are barely touched upon.†

The Contemporaries

The movement of ideas brought on by occultism has grown so extensive in these last years that certain young beginning students do not realize the difficulties which faced Eliphas Lévi in 1850.

It was a time which marked the beginning of the

* In the true etymological sense: *Re-velare*, to symbolize anew.
† Stanislas de Guaita: *On the Threshold of Mystery*, p.66 et seq.

triumph of materialism on all levels: literary, artistic and social. In addition, spiritism threatened to draw its unfortunate and ignorant practitioners into the unproductive paths of mysticism. The mysterious voice, echo of the teachings from hermetic sanctuaries, was however to make itself heard, and Eliphas Lévi was chosen by the Invisible to reveal the principles of the holy Qabalah.

Each time that half-revelations or incomplete teachings come to light, the tradition of esoteric Qabalism, the soul of our Western world, makes itself known and draws to it all generous and enthusiastic minds.

Thus at the moment when Eliphas was writing his remarkable revelations, a great crowd of ambitious individuals from all walks of life adopted the title of magi or initiate, incapable, however, of producing the slightest proof of affiliation with the holy fraternities of the Occident, at least without producing one of those books which assure 'those who know' of the author's connections with what we might call the astral plane.

Today who remembers Paul Auguez or Esquiros, two journalists who claimed to be initiates and made the rounds of the *salons* playing the role of professors in occult science? A few badly written brochures are the only trace which has been left by these audacious men of yesterday.

Among contemporary occultists, who takes notice of Alcide Morin, of his *Revue of Magic* and his *Thirteen Nights*, where all the same are to be found a number of fine ideas?

Who can give full justice to Cahagne, the veritable revelator of spiritism, the curious author of *Arcana of the Future Life*, the ardent magnetist whose superb eloquence has been called smug and middle-class by Allan Kardec, another who none-the-less merits our attention?

Many are the names we might cite to show our epoch the ever-presence of such initiates come out of journalism and incapable of producing any truly initiate work; we could compare them with Esquiros or Paul Augez to demonstrate that the same principals always generate the same laws; but we are not a judge, and time will take care of the task.

Eliphas took great care to emphasize the necessity, for a true occultist, of remaining within a tradition, sanctioned by an order connected with the real teachings of esoteric philosophy. The most striking proof of the truth of this is the fact that names such as Louis Lucas, Desbarolles and Wronski are known and respected today, whereas others such as Auguez and Esquiros and even Alcide Morin are almost entirely forgotten by contemporary occultists.

Such is the law: works which are linked to the principle of truth are given a life whose intensity grows with time, while those born out of division and error are oriented towards death, and the intensity of their annihilation also grows with time.

Eliphas underwent regular initiation into several orders; documents found among his papers testify to this fact, as do his works themselves. What are the principal contemporary manifestations of those initiate centres of yesteryear? We must seek an answer to this question in order to best isolate the influence of Eliphas on our time.

The Traditional Centres of Initiation

It is well known that throughout the ages there have been no greater enemies of the clerical spirit than those men who were actually connected with a real centre of initiation. We need hardly recall the disdain shown by the Therapeutians and Essenians (both initiate in character) towards the Pharisees who were in charge of most of the sacerdotal duties. Later it was the Gnostics who defended the reality of authority against the deceptive illusions of power seized by the clericalism of Christianity, and since, it has always been to Gnosticism or to the Qabalah that the various initiate orders of the West have appealed for that mystic light which illuminates each man born into the world, but that must be sought out from beneath the covering which hides it.

Among the orders which can be linked to Gnosticism let us cite Freemasonry which preserves *the light* in its symbols that remain incomprehensible to F.ˑ. of all grades, just as Israel preserves the Qabalistic hieroglyphs of the Bible without understanding them any more than the Freemasons understand the Gnostic symbols, the foundation of chapters and tribunals.

But just as Israel was made up of three great classes, the Saducees, the Pharisees and the Essenians, the Gnostic tradition, transmitted by the Templars, the alchemist and the Freemasons, includes three instinctive modalities:

1. The lowest, possessing only an instinct for the struggle against clericalism without knowledge of the causes or means of combat, is represented by the Great Orient and the Rite called French.

2. The middle, possessing a certain understanding of the governing laws thanks to the conservation of symbols, of initiate practices and of the hierarchy, and acquainted with the means of attainment, without however a clear perception of the governing cause, is represented by the Rite called Scotch and by the various rites practised in England and the United States.

3. The highest, soaring to the very principle of that *light* sought after so steadfastly by the Freemasons, is manifest in the illuminism which the rite called Martinist represents in France.

To illuminism are attached the Qabalistic order of the Rosicrucians and the Gnostic Church which are the doctrinal, if not historical, continuation of the purest teachings of Gnosticism.

The Templars are represented today historically by the order of Christ of Portugal. As we know, the king of Portugal refused to execute the sentence of death pronounced against the Templars and contented himself with changing the name of the Temple to that of the order of

Christ, keeping the templar cross for its members. Only a white cross was added to the centre of the red cross of the Templars. All dignitaries of the order of Christ are thus *historically* descendants of the Templars. Needless to say, such is not the case doctrinally.

In résumé, the orders which represent in our time the centres of initiation into the esoteric tradition of the Occident are:

1. Freemasonry (excepting the French Rite which has kept only the feeling of the tradition);
2. Martinism;
3. Modern Illuminism: The Kabbalistic Order of the Rosicrucians, the Gnostic Church;
4. The Order of Christ of Portugal.

Such are, in France, the representations of the ancient fraternities, depositaries of esoteric doctrine. Thus when an individual calls himself *initiate*, it is fitting to ask him 'Of what?'

He may reply with works or signs, according to his station; but *he who knows* will never be deceived as to the light, and will be able to discern its divine or human origin. Eliphas Lévi was most closely connected with Illuminism and the Qabalah, as his writings show.

Disciples and Continuators

It would be a mistake to judge the vocation of all modern occultists exclusively upon the influence of Eliphas Lévi. It is especially upon artists and defenders of form that the great Qabalist exercises an almost sovereign control. But contemporary occultism takes its members as much from scientific centres as from literary circles, and it is to Wronski, Court Gébelin and Fabre d'Olivet, even to Luis Lucas, that we must go to find the origin of much of the work of contemporary esoteric thinkers, not to mention the affiliations with initiate fraternities.*

* An occultist's orientation is easily recognizable, as some (the literary) give their names without any title, while the others (the scientific), in conformity with the practice of scientific institutions, add to their name the initiate and other titles which they hold.

Among literary occultists, direct students more or less of Eliphas, let us mention Stanislas de Guaita, Emile Michelet, Alber Jhouney, Joséphine Peladan, René Caillié.

Among occultists of the scientific school and upon whom Eliphas had a real, though secondary, influence, let us cite F. Ch. Barlet, Julien Lejay, Albert Poisson, Marc Haven, Paul Sédir.

Lastly we must also mention those whom the intellectual personality of Eliphas particularly interested: the Baron Spédalieri, Lucien Mauchel, MM. Montaut and Charrot, and Mme Hutchinson, students of the Master.

Stanislas de Guaita

We have always presented the restorer of the Qabalistic order of the Rosicrucians as the most direct continuator of Eliphas Lévi. Of all the students formed by the master, Stanislas de Guaita is uncontestedly the one who has risen to occupy first place, as much by the ardour with which he pursued his study of the Qabalah, as by the magisterial form which encases the profound ideas exposed by the author of *On the Threshold of Mystery*. Already celebrated in literary circles as a poet, Stanislas de Guaita abandoned the cult of the Muse for that of the mysterious Sciences. The work of this young master is now assured of a long existence, and the attacks of envious (and powerless) enemies have not been able to prevail against the authority which arises from work so important and so seriously thought out.

De Guaita has published:

1. *On the Threshold of Mystery:* 1st edition; 2nd edition, considerably enlarged.
2. *The Serpent of Genesis.*

Stanislas de Guaita is an initiate of Illuminism and of Martinism.

Joséphin Peladan

If one could separate, in Eliphas, the artist from the

Qabalist, we would not hesitate to consider M. Joséphin Peladan as one of the most eminent students of the master from an artistic point of view, but as a most mediocre Qabalist. It is in fact impossible for any independent mind not to admire the magnificent form which Peladan has given to the elementary theories of occult science, to such a degree even that the works of the author of *Latin Decadence* have an effect on poets and artists that is as powerful as that of the works of Eliphas himself. But true devotees of the Qabalah can only be shocked by the infantile affirmations presented as the *Cream of Mystery* by M. Peladan, writing that the Zohar is composed of 'a few pages of writing' or positing his ridiculous theory of planetary influence, drawn no doubt from the Chaldeo-Greek tradition. But the form is so fine that in spite of everything the content is saved, and if only ignorants can ascribe to M. Peladan, the Qabalist, this young author has a right to the admiration of all as a writer and artist.

Emile Michelet

Scorning the fashionable success due to an eccentric exterior which hides the vacancy within, putting his entire confidence in the selfless pursuit of Ideal Beauty hidden in the esoteric symbolism of all civilizations, Emile Michelet does not allow his intellectual realizations to appear except after long and patient effort and thought. This no doubt accounts for the very great success of each of his works in the eyes of intellectuals:

1. *Of Esoteric Philosophy in Art.*
2. A series of esoteric lectures to the 'Independent Group for Esoteric Studies' (where Emile Michelet directs esthetic studies).
3. A series of lectures on 'Magic and Love' (in the Salle des Capucines), a veritable masterpiece of science and lofty thinking.

Emile Michelet is an initiate of Illuminism and of Martinism.

Alber Jhouney

M. Alber Jhouney, founder of the mystic review *Star*, is
one of the Qabalists most deeply influenced by Eliphas.
Living a life of retirement in the country, far from quarrels
and rival sects, M. Jhouney spends his time writing very
interesting commentaries on the classics of the Qabalah; at
the present time he is working on an important study of
the Siphra Dzeniuta, that book of mysteries which
occupied Eliphas himself at the beginning of this volume.
Especially interesting is the noble form which M. Jhouney
has given to his thought, and the poetical works of this
young Qabalist deserve a special place in the library of any
occultist devoted to the cult of beauty.

René Caillié

The first in France to direct and maintain a magazine
defending contemporary occultism, the founder of the
Anti-Materialist and the *Review of High Studies*, René
Caillié has had the great honour of propagating the
doctrines of Eliphas Lévi and of winning to them a great
number of admirers. Having just published his *Poem of the
Soul*, where richness of thought shines forth from every
page, René Caillié directs the magazine *Star* with the
greatest competence.

All those acquainted with the sincere faith and generous
heart of René Caillié cannot help but admire the Master
who produced such a disciple.

We have kept our attention most particularly on the more
or less direct students of Eliphas Lévi. As we have already
noted, these disciples are in the main those from literary
milieux; it is no doubt this origin that has allowed them to
penetrate so deeply into the Master's genius.

The as yet unknown work which we are here offering to
the reader was announced by Eliphas Lévi in 1862, at the
beginning of his *Fables and Symbols*, constituting one of

the volumes of the series of Occult Philosophy.

Occult Philosophy

First Series — *Fables and Symbols.*

Second Series — *The Science of Spirits.*

Third Series — *The Book of Mystery,* Siphra Dzeniuta, great sacred book of the Qabalah, translated and explicated for the first time.

Fourth Series — *The Ring of Solomon.*

It is the volume constituting the Third Series which, considerably enlarged, has become the *Book of Splendours* of which the Siphra Dzeniuta is only one part.

As to the *Ring of Solomon,* everything leads us to believe that this title refers to the *Keys,* a volume of engravings commented on in the nine volumes of letters, entirely unpublished and currently in the possession of our friend, Lucien Mauchel.

The authenticity of the present publication is absolutely incontestable.

But it is time to draw to a close.

As we said at the beginning of this study, others better versed in the doctrines of Eliphas Lévi could have undertaken this work and perhaps done a more capable job. But we have always held the Master in the greatest esteem. At the start of our studies in occultism, we even copied a great portion of the finest passages of his works, and the totality of this fills eight thick notebooks. We attribute to this method the little we have retained of this noble doctrine, always distorted by superficial readers or the enemies which Eliphas rather often made.

Thus the reader will excuse any obscurities and weaknesses in this study, considering the sincerity of the admiration which inspired it.

Papus
President of the Independent Group for Esoteric Studies, President of the Supreme Council of the Martinist Order, General Delegate of the Qabalistic Order of the Rosicrucians.

Made in United States
Orlando, FL
27 January 2023